My Father Said Yes

My Father Said Yes

A White Pastor in Little Rock School Integration

Dunbar H. Ogden

Foreword by Archbishop Desmond Tutu

Vanderbilt University Press

NASHVILLE

© 2008 Dunbar H. Ogden
Published by Vanderbilt University Press
All rights reserved
First Edition 2008

12 11 10 09 08   1 2 3 4 5

This book is printed on acid-free paper
made from 30% post-consumer recycled paper.
Manufactured in the United States of America
Design: Dariel Mayer

Frontispiece: Daisy Bates and Dunbar H. Ogden, Jr.,
in the Ogden home, Charleston, West Virginia,
November 30, 1962. Daisy Bates visits in order to
present a copy of her just-published book, *The Long
Shadow of Little Rock*. (Photograph by Ferrell Friend.)

Library of Congress Cataloging-in-Publication Data

Ogden, Dunbar H., III
My father said yes : a white pastor in Little Rock school
integration/ Dunbar H. Ogden ; foreword by Archbishop
Desmond Tutu.—1st ed.
p. cm.
Includes bibliographical references and index.
ISBN 978-0-8265-1592-6 (cloth : alk. paper)

1. Ogden, Dunbar H., Jr., 1902–1978. 2. School integration—
Arkansas—Little Rock—History—20th century. 3. African
American students—Arkansas—Little Rock—History—20th
century. 4. Little Rock (Ark.)—Race relations—History—
20th century. 5. Central High School (Little Rock, Ark.)—
History—20th century. I. Title.
LC214.23.L56033   2007
323.1'19607307677309045—dc22
2007032192

To my wife, Annegret, who
read the newspaper headlines
in Germany two years before
she met her in-laws

> "At crucial moments of choice
> most of the business of choosing
> is already over."
> —Iris Murdoch, *The Sovereignty of Good*

Contents

Illustrations

Foreword

Desmond M. Tutu, Archbishop Emeritus

Cape Town, South Africa, 2004

During 1957–1958, Dunbar Ogden and Daisy Bates formed an unlikely coalition and became the leaders for school integration in Little Rock. He was a white Presbyterian pastor. She was a black journalist who with her husband owned and edited the black newspaper in town.

They supported each other and by example gave each other courage. Each thought the other had a lot of nerve. Many ironies mark that yearlong "collaboration." Ogden was a man of the church while Daisy Bates held little brief for organized religion. But in the end, years later, she said, "He was a true man of God."

The historic moment in Little Rock came about because the Reverend Dunbar H. Ogden, Jr., had visited often and regularly in the homes of the black populace. His role as a churchman gave him that access if he chose to take it. And he did. The wife of a black pastor remembered him vividly: "Some of the white ministers, they knew a lot of black people, but they didn't get down with them like Dunbar Ogden did." No other white pastor or educator had sat on the porches and eaten at the tables of the black community. Ogden understood that the political had to become personal.

Dunbar Ogden and Daisy Bates maintained surprisingly little contact with each other. Yet they had one thing in common: They faced terrible opposition from within their own communities, as well as from outside. Within a year Ogden's congregation would force him to leave town, and within two years Bates's customers would force her to shut down her newspaper. But because of their collaboration, they effected a turning point in American education—the integration of Central High School. Justice begins in school.

Prior to my ordination, I worked as a high school teacher in South Africa. I kept abreast of the 1957–1958 events in Little Rock. As in Little Rock, the rebellion against racism in South Africa erupted around a school issue. In 1976 the apartheid government attempted to impose Afrikaans as the medium of instruction in the black schools. Thousands of children in the black township of Soweto near Johannesburg took to the streets. The regime began to unravel. In 1986 I asked the United Nations for further sanctions against South Africa, and in 1989 the regime fell.

May 9, 1994, marked the birth of the new South Africa. That afternoon I stood on the balcony of the City Hall in Cape Town. For the first time in our history free elections had taken place, and just minutes earlier the Parliament had officially voted. Nelson Mandela, a black man, had been chosen our new president. Dressed in my purple cassock I appeared on the balcony to introduce the newly elected heads of government to the people of South Africa and to the world. I blinked into the sunshine and the faces of a mass of waiting humanity.

A white man, F. M. de Klerk, had been elected one of two deputy presidents (the other was Thabo Mbeki). De Klerk stepped first out onto the balcony. I grasped his hand and held it high. A cheer rose. I heard the hesitancy in the voices for centuries muted by whites and often betrayed by the cruel unpredictability of their own rulers. I saw, as they saw, the hand of the white man, the hand of the oppressor, in my dark-skinned hand. "A miracle has happened." The words spun through my brain. "This is the day of liberation for all of us, black and white together." Suddenly I knew what I had known since childhood: that only through black and white collaboration could justice come into existence. Minutes later I raised the hand of black Deputy President Mbeki and, finally, President Mandela.

I sensed in those seconds with de Klerk's hand in mine—and then Mbeki's and Mandela's—that if our opposition could grow into cooperation, our antagonism would transform into alliance. From opposite sides of the barriers we had striven toward the same goal. Henceforth with personal understanding we could achieve it.

I looked down again into the faces of the crowd. And I knew if we were going to set our nation on a path of justice, then it must come through our children. Pupils of all colors must learn together in the same classroom.

My Father Said Yes illuminates these very issues. It is a remarkable book. Now for the first time Dunbar Ogden's voice can be heard and his actions can be seen in perspective. They dramatize the power of black-white partnership.

Acknowledgments

Without the help of the following people, this book would not have been possible. Peter Barglow, Daisy Bates, Lavinia Browne, William Bynum, Will D. Campbell, David Chappell, Marilyn Chilcote, Walter and Jean Gordon Clancy, Will and Vivian Counts, Deborah De Simone, Richard Dixon, Mimi Dortch, Elizabeth Eckford, Gene Gentry, Ernest Green, Sybil Hampton, Mildred Henderson, Frankie Jeffries, Vernon Kennebrew, Sam McDaniel, Christopher Mercer, Johanna Miller, Kathy Moon, Thelma Mothershed (Wair), Paul W. Ogden, Cameron Olen, Melba Pattillo (Beals), Roy Reed, Terrence Roberts, Mark Segalla, Hezekiah Stewart, Minnijean Brown (Trickey), Rett Tucker, Ann Williams Wedaman, E. Grainger and Frances Williams, Rufus King Young and Yvonne Young, and Carlotta Walls. A special debt of gratitude to Don Campbell for the Little Rock follow-up. And a warm commendation for my research assistant, Gaidi Faraj, who knows his way around libraries and has the instincts of a good sleuth.

For further interview material and other documentation, I am grateful to Harry Ashmore, Cleodis and Sharon Gatson, George Chauncey, Kitty Chism, Dale Cowling, LaVerne Feaster, William Fogleman, Tandy Gilliland, Richard Hardie, James Franklin Henderson, Jr., Kim Holly, Marion Humphrey, Janetta Kearney, James Lawson, Elaine Lechtreck, Christine McBee, Laura Miller, Craig Rains, Beth Roy, and Elizabeth Jacoway Watson.

Two groups of friends have listened critically. Doug McDermott, Jim Stinson, and Robert Sarlós; and Basil DePinto, John Hadsell, Robert McKenzie, and Hugh Wire. In addition, Jim Stinson has given me many days as one of the best line editors in the bookmaking business.

Two other freelance editors have become friends: early on Alison

Owings with her sense of structure and love, and then Marion Abbott with her sense of style and warm-hearted, fun-spirited, and awfully smart guidance in the world of publishing.

At Vanderbilt University Press, Michael Ames believed in the project and helped me to make it the story both of my father and my family. Warm thanks to Sue Havlish for her marketing and to Dariel Mayer, whose touch you see throughout the book.

I wish to extend my most cordial thanks to each of the Little Rock Nine:

Minnijean Brown
Elizabeth Eckford
Ernest Green
Thelma Mothershed
Melba Pattillo
Gloria Ray
Terrence Roberts
Jefferson Thomas
Carlotta Walls

I also wish to thank the freshmen in my annual UC Berkeley class, "Documentary Playmaking." As each student writes an original monologue as a character in the Little Rock story, I keep learning what the integration crisis in Little Rock can mean to new students every year.

How can I express my gratitude to my wife and writing companion? Annegret has freshened every good idea in my books. Her energy never flags. About the oft-repeated family stories in this book, she says, "I've been working hard on this stuff even though I'm sick and tired of it." (She has, however, banned my latest research as dinner table conversation.) And in a family of several writers, she functions as the snappiest title thinker-upper.

I wish to credit the following for photographic material reproduced in this volume: Vivian Counts, for permission to use the photographs by Will Counts that appeared in Will Counts, et al., *A Life Is More than a Moment* (Bloomington: University of Indiana Press, 1999); the *Arkansas Democrat-Gazette*, H. M. Cazad, Ferrell Friend, *Jet*, *Life* (Getty Images), and Paul Ogden.

For further reading, please see Daisy Bates's *The Long Shadow of Little Rock*, and the two meticulously researched and superbly thought-out recent studies: Elizabeth Jacoway's *Turn Away Thy Son* and Grif Stockley's *Daisy Bates*. For what it was like at home and at school for one of the Nine, see Melba Pattillo Beals's very personal *Warriors Don't Cry*.

Timetable

1902	August 15—Dunbar H. Ogden, Jr., born Columbus, Mississippi.
1913 or 1914	November 11—Daisy Lee Gatson (Bates), born Huttig, Arkansas.
1935	March 1—The author, Dunbar III, born, the first of four sons.
1941	Daisy and L. C. Bates move to Little Rock, begin weekly *Arkansas State Press*.
1952	Daisy Bates becomes head of Arkansas NAACP.
1954	Dunbar H. Ogden, Jr., and family move to Little Rock, pastor of Central Presbyterian Church.
1954	May 17—Brown vs. Board of Education.
1955–1956	Montgomery, Alabama, bus boycott.
1957	August 30—Federal court orders Little Rock integration to go forward.
	September 2—Arkansas Gov. Orval Faubus orders National Guard to Central High School.
	September 3—Little Rock schools open.
	September 4—Nine black students attempt to enter Central High. Ogden leads seven of the Little Rock Nine up to National Guard lines. Elizabeth Eckford isolated in mob. All repulsed by National Guard.
	September 23—The Nine go into Central High side entrance with police escort. Mob out front riots.
	September 24—101st Airborne troops enter Little Rock, ordered by President Eisenhower.

September 25—101st Airborne troops escort the Nine to Central High.

October 12—"Day of Prayer" in Little Rock churches.

1958   February 17—Minnijean Brown (one of the Nine) expelled from Central High.

April—Ogden goes to West coast churches, civic clubs for talks about Little Rock.

May 16–18—Ogden goes to Monteagle, Tennessee, Conference.

May 27—Ernest Green (one of the Nine) graduates from Central High. Ogden and M. L. King, Jr., attend. Celebration at home of Daisy and L. C. Bates.

July 18—Officers of Central Presbyterian Church visit Ogden home, demand Ogden's resignation.

September 12—Governor Faubus orders all four Little Rock high schools closed.

c. October 1—Ogden resigns from Central Presbyterian Church, Little Rock, and accepts call to church in Huntington, West Virginia.

October 26—Ogden preaches farewell sermon, Central Presbyterian Church, Little Rock.

Ogdens begin move to Huntington, West Virginia.

1959   October 30—Withdrawal of advertisers forces Daisy and L. C. Bates to stop *State Press.*

1960   June 23—David dies, Rogersville, Tennessee.

1965   March 21–25—Selma to Montgomery, Alabama, march.

1968   April 4—Martin Luther King, Jr., murdered, Memphis, Tennessee.

1978   January 29—Dunbar H. Ogden, Jr., dies, Berkeley, California.

1997   September 19–27—Fortieth anniversary, Central High integration. President Clinton, Gov. Mike Huckabee, and Mayor Jim Daley open Central High doors for the Nine (September 25). Principal Rudolph Howard and Dunbar III attend.

1999   November 4—Daisy Bates dies, Little Rock, Arkansas.

My Father Said Yes

1

"Led by a well-dressed white man in a light suit."

The integration of Central High School in Little Rock, Arkansas, occurred in the fall of 1957. My father, a white Presbyterian pastor, was the man who led the black students up to the lines of the armed National Guard securing the school. The soldiers turned them away. Racist mobs seethed in front of Central High School. President Eisenhower called out the 101st Airborne Division. For a year Little Rock stood at the center of integration history. In the spring of 1958 one of the Little Rock Nine, as the black students came to be known, graduated. Ernest Green had entered as a senior. At Green's graduation my father, together with Daisy Bates, head of the Arkansas NAACP and owner with her husband of the local black newspaper, the *Arkansas State Press*, hosted the young Martin Luther King, Jr. On September 12, 1958, Governor Faubus ordered all four Little Rock high schools closed. By then my father had lost his church and Daisy and L. C. Bates were losing their newspaper. There were many other losses.

Forty years later, in 1997, I was invited to Little Rock to represent my late father at the integration anniversary celebration. There I would talk with original participants.

Unlike many of the other people who took part in these events, my father never wrote of his experiences. I am doing it for him now.

This account is based on fourteen hours of interviews with my father that I taped in 1977. After my father died in 1978, my mother listened to the tapes and corrected the transcripts I had had made, checking the transcriptions of my father's words, supplying names and dates, and correcting spellings where necessary. Eventually I tape-recorded an additional dozen hours separately with my mother; conducted interviews with my two surviving brothers; and interviewed some five dozen people in Little Rock, including Daisy Bates (author of *The Long Shadow of Little Rock*), Elizabeth Eckford (one of the Nine, who in 1957 become the most famous girl in the world for a year), and Rufus King Young (black pastor and eventual president of the integrated Ministerial Association). I have also drawn upon the contents of eleven file-cabinet drawers of manila file folders filled by my father—a meticulous record keeper and newspaper clipper. In this account, I have often let Daisy Bates and her husband, L. C. Bates, speak through their weekly *State Press*. And I have attempted to walk my own tightrope of recall between verifiable fact and faulty memory.

Different from Other Fathers

As a child I knew my father was different from other fathers. When I came down with the measles, he sat by my bedside and read Shakespeare's *Henry V* aloud to me, every word of it, inserting his own running social and political commentary. I was ten.

He was always bringing unusual people to our home for lunch or dinner—the president of Princeton Seminary, a local black pastor with his New York Opera Company singer sister, a convicted felon just out on parole and turning to my father to help him find a job. My mother knew always to have an extra plate ready.

Every day my father talked about what was going on in the world. He'd sit at the dining room table clipping newspaper and magazine articles and discussing what was in them—the very clippings that were to lie in unopened boxes in my basement after his death. He remained steadily vocal in his opinions. Where these were political, he usually disagreed with my mother. She voted consistently Republican and he consistently Democrat. But they never argued. Every Sunday afternoon—from grade school through high school—he took me and my brother David to services he held regularly in the state mental institution and the "lime-grinding plant"—a state prison where the prisoners quarried rock for road building. He'd have the two of us play our clarinets as part of his service.

From a traditional upbringing in the Deep South in the early part of the twentieth century, my father, like my grandfather, became a Presbyterian minister. He pastored his first congregation among the mountain hollows of North Carolina, traveling around his "home-mission" riding his horse Dixie. In 1930 he went to a church in Pikeville, Kentucky, where he met my mother. She had come to Pikeville College and the local schools as a music teacher. They married in 1933, and he soon took a church in Portsmouth, Ohio. They had three boys: me (b. 1935), David (b. 1936), and Jonathan (b. 1938). In 1940 we moved to Staunton, Virginia. A fourth son arrived, Paul (b. 1949). My father answered the call to First Presbyterian of Staunton at a salary of $4,500, and left eleven years later at the same salary. He was always too proud to ask for more, even though $1,000 went every year toward Jonathan's schooling at Central Institute for the Deaf in St. Louis.

My father's pastorate at the First Presbyterian Church of Staunton, Virginia (1940–1951), ranked as a distinguished position. Joseph R. Wilson, Woodrow Wilson's father, had served it. Woodrow Wilson was born there in the manse. Traditionally, the minister of First Presbyterian also occupied the presidency of Mary Baldwin College, across the street from the church. That tradition had been discontinued two generations before my father's arrival. Instead, the minister of First Presbyterian automatically became the secretary of the board. My father accepted the position. He was on his way up.

And then one of his bouts of depression felled him. That too constituted part of his Southern heritage, a genetic inheritance.

Depression

My father spent seven months in recovery in the medical center of Johns Hopkins, receiving electroshock and other treatments. Our family spread apart: I went to Davidson College in North Carolina, my brother David to Hampden-Sydney College in Virginia, Jonathan to Central Institute for the Deaf in St. Louis, and my mother with two-year-old Paul to her mother's in Springfield, Ohio. Released from Johns Hopkins half a year later, my father spent a year in the northwest Arkansas home of his brother Fred, a doctor in Fayetteville. Then he took a tiny rural pastorate in Pea Ridge, Arkansas. My family rejoined him there.

One summer day my father led me out to a barn behind the manse (pastor's house) in Pea Ridge. I was home from college. We walked through the big, rectangular door opening into the barn. Fresh, clean straw lay everywhere. Pieces of cattle rope. Light streamed in through high roof windows. At roof level a six-by-twelve beam ran the length of the barn. My father stopped, stood for a moment, and pointed up at the rafters. "I used to come out here and stand right on this spot and look up and think where I could find a good thick rope. I'd think about throwing it up over that beam and hanging myself from it. Just ending my life that way. One morning I even made a hangman's noose. Do you know how to tie a hangman's noose? We used to tie all kinds of knots in Boy Scout camp when I was a scout-master. A hangman's noose was our favorite, a sort of joke. But then I'd think about what that would do to Mother over there in the house. When she'd come out and find me. And I knew I had to keep going."

I do not know what prompted him to have that conversation with me. Telling me all that made me hugely uncomfortable. I did not want to hear it. When he grew vulnerable in my presence or when he wanted to tell me about his vulnerabilties, or when tears welled up in his eyes, I wanted to run. At the same time, I felt guilty for feeling nervous. I wanted to put my hand on his shoulder, to comfort him—maybe I did, I don't remember—all the while aching to get out of there. We did not have the habit of giving each other hugs. I felt so sorry for him. I felt puzzled by my emotional inertia. I could have comforted him had he not been my father, if he had been a stranger perhaps. To this day I am still puzzled by this wrenching ambivalence in me.

Perhaps it stems from a conflict between the parent and the pastor that I knew. I use the word "pastor" to single out his public and private church-related authority: his role in conducting services, in performing weddings and baptisms and funerals, in comforting and guiding others. We felt this pastoral role at home, where his presence always brought church business with it, where he defined his hours by church meetings (after supper he always left the house for some church-connected occasion), and where he punctuated his talk with names of church people and details of church events.

My father was a fixer, and a man of action. So was my mother. When he and my mother had a totally deaf son, and then another, they set out to do something about it. When each deaf boy was a pre-schooler, my mother constructed a plan of education at home; then when the first deaf boy reached school age, my parents searched throughout the United States and interviewed scores of people to find the best school for training deaf children to speak and lip-read. My parents got both boys into the school they chose. The costs were way beyond their means. And yet they did it. They struggled for scholarships, and they overcame enormous heartache at sending these two children a thousand miles away from home. Yet, there my father stood in that barn, caught in the throes of a depression, and he could not fix it, and I felt a paralysis that kept my arms against my sides.

He had inherited the plague of depression—it blighted his family. He knew "the pit of hell," his term for a period of depression. "I wouldn't wish it on a dog," he'd often say. Clinical depression. He sank four times: 1922, 1930, 1951, 1974. Gifted with detailed recall that was legendary among his school classmates and later-life associates, he revisited in his memory all past occurrences either in the bright light of healthy day or in the shadows of the pit. He said that he remembered past events during a depression period as if they had unrolled behind a kind of mist.

In the Pea Ridge barn he kept a lawnmower that he used to cut the half acre of grass around the little church manse. He did that for therapy. Physical activity had been prescribed toward his recovery. He hated it: making pottery or weaving rugs at Johns Hopkins, or now gardening. Walking he liked. But not these endless, dead-end tasks that called up in his mind, he said to me, the mule in the cane mill that he as a boy watched go round and round all day, turning the millstone. Then and now that image cast a pall over his whole being, he said. Pushing the lawnmower, digging the soil, he would sink listless into the terror of mindless, meaningless, hopeless existence.

I have often thought that the full horrors of that plague's visitation can be known only to those who inherit its numbing, maddening disorientations and spiritual nauseas. My father tried frequently to describe it to me. I can only report pieces of what he said, not the anguish of his saying it. He knew the sensation of "going through the motions" when in a public situation—my father's expression—and when in private, he knew the conviction that even a gesture of love from a wife or child demonstrates that one cannot be loved. He knew the weeping and the muttering of nonsense syllables to comfort himself, a tortured alien in a godforsaken world.

Dunbar Hunt Ogden, Jr., and Dorothy Coblentz Ogden,
Roaring River State Park, Missouri, spring 1954.

Some mornings on that summer visit with my parents in Pea Ridge, I would catch a glimpse of him through the open door of the bathroom, his face lathered, standing shaving with a safety razor, and I would hear him muttering Greek-like nonsense syllables at the mirror—"mongeltoid, eaglebleakstoid"—punctuated now and again by a deep sigh and a catching of the breath before mumbling on. Once when he saw me, he said, "Don't let this bother you. It gives me relief."

In 1954 my father went to the pastorate of Central Presbyterian in Little Rock, Arkansas. It was located a few blocks from Central High School. He said to me later that when he accepted the call to the Little

Four Ogden boys, Little Rock, Christmas 1954. Left to right: David (with "George," the white rat he brought from college for Paul), Dunbar III holding Paul, and Jonathan. (Photograph by Dorothy Ogden.)

Rock church, he was still forcing himself. He had to continue "just going through the motions." But then, he told me, the pall of his depression finally lifted in the summer of 1955. He could even recall the exact day.

By 1957 he was fifty-five years old, and he felt ready to step back into the Presbyterian limelight. But all through the crisis events that were to come, my mother worried that he would fall back into the depression of the early 1950s from which he had just emerged.

By 1957 my father, thin-skinned by depression to overwhelming empathy for any downtrodden person and himself a man of action, had just regained a peak of confident energy. I suspect that when he came out of a depression, the feeling of "empathy" toward another human being meant something stronger for him than for most of the rest of us. Perhaps he felt something more intense for someone downtrodden, disadvantaged, threatened, or in pain: the experience that we call "compassion." When face-to-face with such a person, an almost uncontrollable force could take him over, even possess him. And he would take action. All of his life he refused every invitation to visit church missions in Korea and India because, he said, he simply could not stand to see the poverty and the suffering in the streets.

My father said that on the telephone he could always recognize the voice of a depressed person. Because of him, I too can tell a depressed person by his voice, how it sinks and drags and becomes very low and can fade in mid-sentence. How the voice slithers and spills out of the mouth. I too can hear depression on the telephone. When my father flourished in good health, his voice gripped his words firmly.

Unprotested Injustice

By 1977 my father had semiretired to Berkeley, California, where he took a position as associate pastor of a local Presbyterian church. Every other morning for a period of two weeks that spring, I would take my tape recorder and go over to my parents' cottage. And I would sit with my father on one side of me, my mother on the other, and a small microphone on the table, the tape recorder located down on the seat of a chair beside me so it would not distract us.

I decided to begin with September 4, 1957, asking him for every detail that he could recall, and then to reach back to his childhood experiences with African Americans in the Deep South. For each session he would shower, shave, and dress in jacket and white shirt, sometimes putting on a tie. He would start by folding his muscular hands on the table—immaculate as always with nails trimmed—and would wait thoughtfully for me to start asking. At seventy-five he retained his head of thick black hair, brushed back and now slightly peppered with white.

My father's middle name recalls his great-grandfather, David Hunt, owner of more than two thousand slaves and four large plantations in Mississippi. Family lore insists that the plantation houses boasted doorknobs and hinges of silver, as well as draperies and cut-glass chandeliers brought over by boat from Europe and on up the Mississippi, to be unloaded at Natchez. Both of my father's grandfathers and a step-grandfather fought for the Confederacy as officers. One spent time in a Union prison, one was wounded, and one was killed. Another great-grandfather sat on the Supreme Court of the State of Louisiana. Behind them lurked Ogden-related governors of New Jersey and North Carolina.

My grandfather, the first Dunbar H. Ogden (the "Dunbar" from a family branch), became a Presbyterian minister. In 1900 he took his first pastorate in Columbus, Mississippi, the town where Tennessee Williams was born in 1911. Tennessee's grandfather was the rector of the local Episcopal church down the street from my grandfather's church. Eventually my grandfather served a roll call of distinguished churches in Southern Presbyterianism: in Knoxville, Atlanta, Louisville, Mobile, and New Orleans. He led the struggle to reunite the church after the Civil War. Davidson College, Marysville College, and Southwestern University bestowed honorary doctoral degrees on him.

My father, Dunbar H. Ogden, Jr., was born in Columbus, Mississippi, in 1902, and was brought up (he would say "reared") in Knoxville and Atlanta, where he attended Boys' High School. Each summer during his childhood his mother would take him, the oldest, and his younger siblings, eventually seven children in all, back to Columbus, Mississippi, for summer vacations in their grandmother's home. Black maids helped to manage the children on this annual train trek. My father's earliest memories were filled with black people. Mattie, "a fat, genial Negro woman" (my Uncle Warren would tell me), attended at all seven home births. Black servants were part of the Ogden household and the households of the grandparents. A yardman, coachman, cook, and two maids comprised the Columbus grandmother's staff.

"One of my earliest childhood memories," my father often repeated during my boyhood and later, "is of a cane mill that must have been near Columbus. I remember seeing Negroes bending and working, the same motion over and over, and I remember standing there beside a mule walking around and around treading the cane, tied to a post, his head down, just around and around that post hour after hour. And as I look back on it, I had an overwhelming sadness, a compassion for this mule. I wanted to stop it. To feed it. It was dry, dry. To give it something to drink. Maybe in my mind those Negroes were like the mule."

As he and my mother and I sat in their living room at the card table in 1977 with the tape-recorder spools spinning, my father repeated this story, chanting the word "dry" half a dozen times, choking as he said it. I could hear in his voice and see in his face that he was feeling himself plodding around and around in those tracks, desperately parched.

It was in a period of depression that he had first told me, as a grade-schooler, the mule-at-the-cane-mill story, when he had "to keep going through the motions." As I watched him now during my 1977 interview, it dawned on me that as long as I had known him, I had often seen him moved by extreme compassion. It would happen when he looked someone in the face who was physically suffering, and particularly when face-to-face with someone who was ragged, dirty, in dire poverty. Tears would well up in his eyes. I would see him reach out and take an old man by the hand—often an old black man on the porch of his shanty—my father holding his hand in both hands. As a child I could accept his compassion, but as a man of forty-two during that 1977 interview, it embarrassed me. I found myself shifting around in my chair and quickly changing the subject. It still made me nervous to see my father start to choke up. As I go over the interviews now, I am sorry that I would do that.

He also took pleasure in shocking people with graphic stories: "In Columbus there was a mortuary," he said, as if picturing the scene in front of him. "I don't know whether they served black and white, or just the black people, or what. It had a window in front. A very simple sort of place, no frills about it. But one thing they had in their window was the foot of a black person which was cut off right above the ankle. Then it had been embalmed and the skin drawn together and kind of sewed up and tied. I would stop and look at that, and it had a sort of horror, and yet a fascination for me."

He paused. He was feeling the horror. He continued appalled, "I would look at it and I would think, 'That foot really belonged to somebody, and it was a black man. He walked on that foot and he doesn't have it anymore.'"

He was envisioning it. I remembered that very same fixed stare into the middle distance that could come over him while he was preaching. Standing in the pulpit he would start telling a story, both hands open in front of him, making a biblical scene graphic to his congregation—becoming emotionally involved with the characters, feeling with them and for them.

During one of our Berkeley tape-recording sessions, he recalled romping in a river near his grandmother's Mississippi home. "We boys played at the Tombigbee River," he started. "A white friend named Jim and I played with a Negro boy who lived on a plantation owned by Jim's father. Jim called the boy 'Snowball.' Jim's father had 'given' Snowball to Jim. It released the Negro boy from going out to hoe cotton. We were about eight. We went swimming, and one of the things we did we scuffled and tussled and tried to hold each other underwater until one raises his hand. That means 'I give up.'" My father was raising his hand, reenacting the scene.

"Okaaaay," he sang out, in his imagination still at the river. "Then you can come up. I had the feeling that Snowball could have won over us, but he would not. Jim would hold him under a long time. Jim was mean to him a lot of times. But he'd just take it, and laugh, or have a sort of noncommittal attitude. The main thing was, he didn't want trouble with Jim. He was Jim's 'nigger.'" My father tried to say the last sentence in an even-toned, matter-of-fact way, as perhaps any local plantation owner would have said it. My father hated the word "nigger." A shock went through me when I heard him use it. Then I understood that he had said the sentence without putting stress on that word—as a liberal non-Southern civil rights propagandist might—because he wanted me to hear in his level-voiced, offhand manner the way in which this expression—and his story—illustrated an accepted way of life. If I grasped that in his telling, then I would grasp his outrage at the hideous treatment of people, made the more heinous in his view because nobody questioned it. While he was telling the story, he wanted me to experience his shock in awakening as a boy to this unprotested injustice. He also wanted me to feel his present sense of outrage at what he had witnessed back then.

For the same reasons—and in that same level voice—he brought up an event from his school days in Atlanta. "Another time I was on my way home from school, where I would pass by a dry cleaning shop with some machinery outside. That was in Atlanta [his father was a minister there from 1909–1918]. One day a little Negro boy went skipping by there. He might have been seven or eight. I might have been twelve. Some of the men were hanging around outside, having lunch or something. One of them, maybe the foreman, called out to the boy, 'Hey, come over here. Now you come right over here.' When the Negro boy did, the foreman grabbed him by the neck, pulled back his shirt, picked up one of those oil cans with a long spout like they use on the railroad, stuck it down the boy's back, and squirted him full. 'Hey, that'll oil up the little nigger!' The boy ran off crying."

He wanted me to hear his startled revulsion then, his opening consciousness of inhumanity around him, as well as his present revulsion.

Then he told me an event that had seared itself into his memory. "After we moved to Atlanta, a Victoria Sleigh worked for us," he said. "She was our cook for a while. One day my mother asked her, she said, 'How do you feel about it that some of us are white and some of us are black? Do you mind having been born like that?' And she is reported to have said, she says, 'Miz Ogden, I tell you I would be willing to be skinned all the way from the top of my head down to my toes, stripped of all my skin, if I could be white.' "

He stopped. I heard the slight whir of the tape recorder, recording no sound. My mother didn't move. Once more my father turned and stared me hard in the eyes, to make sure I was getting his outrage at the horrors he was delivering with his stories. Sometimes he would become so tense with emotion that he could not stop the telling. His mouth would just keep going, repeating still another story.

Sitting at that table with him, I began to realize that he was a man split. On the one hand, he was holding on to an encyclopedia of details and names painted over with heartfelt nostalgia. On the other hand, he could not accept all this "Southern gentility." And step by step during his growing up he had awakened to its callous treatment of a people, to injustices perpetrated by people he loved. I remember a childhood visit in the home of an aunt, his sister, where my father held forth—at length, for the benefit of assembled young cousins—about family oddities in the old days that bordered on the reprehensible. Suddenly and totally out of character, his sister reprimanded him in fierce tones that in another mood she would have called "unladylike." "Dunbar, I don't want to hear another word out of you critical of our parents," she said, shutting down our visit.

Yet during these taped conversations with me, he spoke often and always with great fondness about his Southern relatives. One who made an undimmed impression on him was an older, married cousin who lived across the state from the home of the Columbus, Mississippi, grandmother. There my father said he experienced his happiest visits. "My cousin Stanard had a big Mississippi plantation near the Arkansas border, just north of Greenwood. I went to visit when I was a young boy and as a teenager, several times. He had acquired some eleven thousand acres by then.

"Stanard Equen and his wife had a true, warm home. Cousin Stanard worked very hard, with hands on. He did lots of hunting—had parties of men—bobcats, snakes, all sorts of wildlife was still plentiful, and dangerous. He was what you'd call a man's man, he was OK. He had a lot of good, likable qualities in him, about average height, reddish chestnut hair they called 'chatin'—Creole patois, I think—and a twinkle in his blue eyes. In later life he was what ladies would call a very delightful gentleman."

My father would start remembering and there was no stopping him. During earlier times like this, my brother David and I—as captive youngsters at the dining room table—would roll our eyes and start pitching scraps of food under the table for Mickey the dog. This time, however, I was listening intently, feeling guilty about all the times I had let his Southern family stories go in one ear and out the other.

"On one visit, my younger sister Grace Augusta—a year younger than me—and Stanard's much younger half sister, Virginia, came along. One afternoon we decided to go horseback riding. They had house servants too, and all you had to do was say you wanted to go and you could go. There were these lanes between the ten-acre parcels, with narrow little stretches of woodlands, and it's so easy to get lost down there, you see, if the cotton is high. And then there are some main lanes, a main lane to the big house. Maybe you get out there and you can't find how to get back. This one goes that way, and that one that way." With his open hand my father traced the plantation lanes on the card table between us.

His tones were gentling into Southern cadences and a smile had crept into his voice. "Well, my sister and I thought we'd have a little fun with Virginia. We whipped up our horses to tease her and we lost her. We just thought, she'll follow. Well, she didn't, she didn't make the effort. I guess she didn't care. We lost her. We looked around but we couldn't find her. We thought she can't really get lost, but I was pretty worried. We jogged on our horses toward the plantation house laughing and talking.

"When we rode up late that afternoon, Stanard was there, and Stanard says, 'Where's Virginia?' I said, 'Oh, she's back there somewhere.' He said, '**Where** is Virginia?' We said, 'She's coming along after a while, she'll be . . . .' He said, 'Do you mean you just rode off and left her? Do you know what kind of a place this is? You realize we live in a place where we've got just three white families here. We've got the storekeeper, and we have myself, and we have the overseer. There are three white families on thousands of acres, and we've got hundreds of Nigras out there, and there are always some of those people you can't trust. There are some bad-acting niggers out there. . . .' "

My father cringed as he was saying that. He said, "Stanard really blew his stack: When somebody in the family went from 'Nigra' to 'nigger,' you knew they were mad. They called blacks 'Nigras,' a sort of genteel word, and so did my parents."

Then my father picked up the story. "By this time Cousin Stanard had spotted the stable boy. 'My God, **saddle my horse**.' And he tore out of the yard. A couple of other men who happened to be there rode out in other directions. Anyway, he found her pretty quick, and brought her in."

Sitting beside my father in his California living room with the tape recorder turning, I saw Cousin Stanard's fear and fury as the muscles bulged in my father's neck. At the same time I saw, in the way my father raised his hand and let it fall on the tabletop, that at that time his cousin's shock had caught him totally by surprise, my father a young teenager merely playing a prank. As a child, when I would see that easy, prankish mood come across his face, I myself would feel a happiness—that I could let my guard down, and not have to mind my behavior or what I said.

"Now, I don't know whether Stanard's fear and anger were justified or not," he went on matter-of-factly. "In those days black men wouldn't dare even raise their eyes in the presence of a white woman, or if they didn't have a completely humble attitude pretty much all the time in the presence of a white woman, they could lose their life for it." My father was always explaining along with his telling, as he did when he would sit at the breakfast table and read the Bible to us.

Once more he looked me in the eye and held to an even, level tone, so that I would absorb the indignation that had grown in him since childhood at what he had experienced as practiced in black-white relations. At the same time, he was reigniting his own flashes of recognition, those drastic moments when as a boy something sparked inside him, some fire alarm went off in his brain for the first time delivering the warning that something was wrong. He was telling me the startling events from his youth that had shocked him into looking with different eyes at the behavior of blacks toward whites, and whites toward blacks: in his grandmother's home and garden; in the shops of Columbus, Mississippi; and in the streets of his boyhood homes in Knoxville, Atlanta, and Louisville. These warning jolts made him see uncommon things in common life that others could not see—and they upset him.

From my earliest awareness of my father, I knew his obsession with fair play. It was as if he had fingertips sandpapered to extremes of sensitivity whenever he touched an action that was unfair and unjust. As a child I knew that nothing could anger him more quickly and more vehemently than to see someone "mistreating" (the word he used) an animal or, especially, "mistreating another human being."

It was this familiar undercurrent of rage that started to shape his sentences as he went on with his story about his Cousin Stanard's plantation. "But this fear in Stanard, I don't know whether it was justified, or whether he knew better than I. I didn't feel that Virginia was in all that danger, but Stanard was very suspicious of what they'd do to his teenage half sister. Well, he found her and brought her in."

My father conjured up another episode that had turned his head around. "One morning—that was on another visit to Cousin Stanard's plantation—Stanard walked into the kitchen where his wife was giving me breakfast. 'I've been having a little trouble with Bill over there,' Stanard said, raising his chin toward the sharecroppers' cabins out beyond the plantation house. Just how many there were back then, I don't know. By the late 1940s there were 120 cabins. Anyway, he said, 'I've got to go over there and see Bill. I've got to straighten that nigger out. You want to come along?' He could change so quickly from being so gracious to his wife and relatives when he was pleased with someone to this kind of anger when something or someone displeased him. And to my surprise he goes over to the closet and gets out this big holster and a rather large handgun and leather gun belt. You've seen them in Western movies.

" 'I'm the one that knows how to do it,' he said. He grabbed the belt and slung it around his waist and buckled it up. The barrel of the pistol reached through the holster halfway down his thigh. The thing was huge. It rode up and down on his hip as he walked. We went out to his Dodge. He flung the pistol onto the back seat, and we climbed in. We slammed down some dusty roads past cornfields and cotton fields. The car was a convertible. He could tear around there in it. He didn't ride his horses very much because he could get so much quicker from one part of the plantation to another in the Dodge.

"The morning August sun had started to heat up its metal and leather. Thirty yards off the road stood an unpainted board shanty. It may have had two or three rooms. Cousin Stanard pulled over. A black woman was sitting on the steps of the porch fanning herself.

" 'Where's Bill?' shouted my cousin.

" 'Well, he's 'roun' here somewhere, Mistah Stanard,' she said.

" 'You go tell him to get out here. And quick. Tell Bill to come out here.' A hardness hung in his voice. The black woman struggled to her feet and disappeared into the house.

"Then here comes this man out, middle-aged black man. He stands there on the steps of his shanty.

"Cousin Stanard gets out and reaches over, picks up the pistol, and starts fumbling with it. The black man sees the handgun.

" 'Come down here,' shouts my cousin Stanard. The black man walks a few steps out to the road and stops by the car, a careful distance from the weapon. His head and shoulders slumped, dusty and torn clothes hanging on him. He just stands, his thick hands by his sides. 'Why haven't you got on better with your cotton here? Why haven't you got your wife and children out there hoeing? You aren't even through with your second cotton chopping, and it's gonna be time to start chopping those weeds again. What's the matter with you, anyway? And your wife and those kids?'

" 'Yas suh, yas suh, yas suh, Mistah Stanard, yas suh. We'll do it. Yas suh. We'll sure do it. Yas suh.'

" 'Now I mean it. You get on back. We'll be back to check on you. All right, Bill.' Cousin Stanard gets in the Dodge, pitches the weapon in the backseat, and steps on the gas. The last I saw of Bill through the dust, he hadn't moved.

"A few minutes later my cousin relaxed into his familiar, congenial self. 'I really straightened him out, didn't I,' said Stanard. 'I guess he knows I put the fear of God in him, all right.' "

Nowhere during my tape-recording sessions with my father did his inner conflict surface more vividly. Sitting there in his Berkeley cottage, he was feeling a huge affection for Stanard and the plantation of his youth, and an abiding nostalgia for his grandmother and her Columbus, Mississippi, home, even as this affection and nostalgia clashed with his perceptions of injustice toward blacks. This nostalgia was also tainted by the guilt that emanated from a shocked loss of innocence. My father was becoming aware as a child, and he wanted me to understand.

When he started to tell his stories from his youth, his words softened into the Southern sounds and rhythms of his accustomed role as storyteller and Bible reader. Yet even in his attempts to imitate the speech of one of his uneducated characters, he could not quite glide into the Mississippi accents of his childhood neighbors or verbally reproduce "Bama" or Louisiana "Bayou" or Arkansas "redneck." No matter how much his eyes told me he had entered into each scene, his mouth never slipped into actual "Delta" speech. Since my earliest days I knew his tones before I knew his words. In our home he never missed a chance to correct our pronunciation. At one point my little brother David started saying "quippery" instead of "slippery," referring to the bottom of a local swimming pool. My mother told me she thought it "so cute." But over my mother's objections my father refused to let it stand and at the dinner table he would work with little David on his "sl." He also took every cue to pull a dictionary from a shelf (we had one in every room) and look up a word with us. I can still hear his ringing declaration: "That is the *first* pronunciation."

Not until my college days in North Carolina did I become conscious of class differences revealed by "hick" and "redneck" Southern speech. I am sure that early on from my parents I picked up attitudes toward people based on the way they talked, especially differences between what my parents would call "educated" and "uneducated" people. When answering the telephone in our Staunton, Virginia, home, I would sometimes summon my father with, "Dad, the janitor down at the church wants to talk with you," when in fact it was the chief church elder (a white owner of a local dry-goods store). From the way they talked on the phone, using the same accent, I could not tell the difference. My father would say to us, "Go and listen to the way your mother talks. She speaks perfectly." (My mother had grown up in Ohio.) However, there was not a hint of uneducated dialect in my father's carefully groomed speech, a genteel "Southern" demanded by his own parents and fostered by the so-called debating societies at his North Carolina college. In his day, students coveted membership in these exclusive clubs more than in any other organization on campus, societies that each owned its own ancient building, where my father had won gold medals and elected offices.

During the next tape-recording session, my father told me a story from his college days about a picture he and others had posed in for the yearbook. At no time in our lifelong relationship did I ever feel him cringe inwardly so much at something he had done. He said, "But just to show you how blind I was to other situations, when I was a student at Davidson College, in North Carolina, one time we staged a mock lynching, a sort of stunt so we could take a picture of it and put it in the college yearbook. And it's right there. We paid a black man, one of the janitors, I don't know, a dollar, to pose with us, and we all dressed up in our ROTC uniforms and what all. We stood him by a big tree with a rope hanging from it. In the picture I have

Mock lynching staged by Davidson College students "as a prank" for the Davidson College, North Carolina, yearbook, 1920. In later years Dunbar H. Ogden, Jr., claimed to have participated. His name is not one of those listed, but is he at the far left brandishing a pistol?

my ROTC pistol out, and I am crouching down and threatening him with it. We thought it was all just hilarious, a prank. You can look in the 1920 yearbook and there it is. I've since thought what a tragedy it was that he was subjugated to the point he wasn't aware of his own humiliation."

At what moment had this event metamorphosed in my father's mind from prank into guilty horror? At what point in his life did he come to realize that he was participating in a way of life that he deplored? I do not know. As I review our interviews and what else I know of his life, I do not come across a lightning flash of recognition.

What I do discover is that years later in Little Rock, all at once he did not have to stand there and just let it happen as it had in his boyhood days. He could step in and stop it.

2

"Blood will run in the streets."

Fall 1957

On the night of September 2, 1957, the day before school opening, Governor Orval Faubus ordered an armed detachment of the Arkansas National Guard to surround Central High School in Little Rock, Arkansas. At 10:15 p.m. he went on television to tell the people of Arkansas that he had prayed about the matter and acted out of dire necessity—because of "evidence of disorder and threats of disorder." Otherwise, according to the Daisy Bates version in her *Long Shadow of Little Rock*, Faubus warned that "blood will run in the streets" of Little Rock. Different news agencies reported his prediction in milder terms, quoting his stated fears about "the harm that may occur on the morrow." In any case, immediately following the broadcast the school board instructed the nine black students who were preparing to enroll to stay away.

The school opened all white on the morning of September 3. Later that day, Federal Judge Ronald Davies ordered integration to start the next day, September 4.

By the night of September 3, Daisy Bates's back was to the wall. She had engineered the next day's entry of the nine black students into Central High after painstakingly persuading some of their parents. All the while, black parents and their children were hearing that if the children attempted to enroll, they would be murdered. A white mob had gathered at the school that morning. The KKK swore "bloodshed if necessary." The black parents had to stay away, ordered Superintendent Virgil Blossom, or their presence might foment a riot. And there would be zero police protection. Was she sending the children out there to die?

That was when Daisy Bates called my father. He remembered her asking him, "Reverend Ogden, would you gather together a group of white ministers and accompany our nine boys and girls to Central High tomorrow?"

The impending integration of Central High was already looming large in my father's mind. The previous Sunday he had preached at Central Presbyterian Church on Paul's letter to the Colossians, calling his sermon "Christ Supreme." In his sermon notes he wrote, "Christ is the head of every Christian community and of all people as they mingle with each other—*giving* what each group has to give, and receiving what each group can receive." He underscored "giving." On the same page he wrote, "Let us ask for God's guidance in the matter of *INTEGRATION* in our public schools in this year of 1957—particularly in Central High School of Little Rock on day after tomorrow, Tuesday, September 3rd." He did not yet know it would be September 4th.

Daisy Bates called my father because he was president of the interracial Ministerial Association. She was desperate. She thought that perhaps a gathering of respected white citizens from the community would serve to protect the children the next day. Otherwise they were going out there defenseless to face a mob. The mob that morning at school opening had numbered eight hundred. They had milled about while some two thousand white students had streamed over to Central High, the crew-cut boys in jeans and sport shirts, here and there a cigarette pack rolled into the sleeve of a white T-shirt, books on their hips. The wavy-haired girls in fresh blouses, here and there flaring skirts and dresses and penny loafers, clutching books and pencil cases in their arms, all turned out.

In our home that night Daisy Bates's call came as a lightning strike. It shook my father in a way that nothing before had. Decades later, in my interview with him, he would quote the conversation verbatim. "Well now, Mrs. Bates," he said. "Do you think this is the business of the church? Do you think it's part of the work of religion to participate in a movement that might be thought of as more political and social than of a churchly nature? Don't you think it's possible it will be said of the ministers that they've gotten a little too dramatic,

Dunbar H. Ogden, Jr., with his rare copy (1585) of the Geneva Bible, called the "Breeches Bible," Huntington, West Virginia, December 3, 1959. (Photograh by H. M. Cazad.)

going out there and walking with the Negro children? Aren't there other ways they could help better?" She disagreed firmly.

My father said he would call her back in five or ten minutes. He talked it over with my mother and together they prayed, while Daisy Bates waited, tense. Years later my father reflected: "I thought at the time, for some reason, this may be a stepping stone if I can do something here. Central Church was very humdrum, pedestrian, and unexciting. Maybe doing something like this will be a way that I can go on to something that's really challenging." Both of my parents used the word "providential" with some frequency. They did that night.

My father telephoned back with a promise to contact as many clergy as he could. He said he would meet with the students the next morning before they started for school, but he did not know whether he would go with them.

"I don't know how many ministers I called, but quite a few," my father told me years later, "perhaps a dozen, the men I thought most likely to go, and every one of them declined to go with me except one, Colbert Cartwright, who was minister of the Pulaski Heights Christian Church." The others, my father said to me, offered one of two excuses: "If I go out there tomorrow morning, it will split apart my congregation and destroy my effectiveness with my people." Or they said, "My wife won't let me." Meaning, my father thought: I might get hurt. Two other white ministers visiting town learned of my father's predicament and volunteered to go "if, in your judgment," they told him, "you think it's right."

After making his calls to the Little Rock clergy, my father kept asking himself, "What should I do?" He remembered, "Before going to bed that night I asked myself and I asked God in prayer. It wasn't clear in my mind whether this was right and whether it was best or not. I don't know how much was just the fear of getting hit in the head with a rock or bottle or getting hit in the face with someone's fist."

He sweated all through the night (he would have said "perspired"), half-dreaming of truckloads of men in plaid shirts and hats and jeans rumbling into town, rows of men from Crossett and the "black-belt" delta bristling with rifles. Pickups with Brownings and Remingtons racked across their rear windows. Later he told me he dreamed about faces, mouths pulled open, not drop-jawed open but wrenched at a slant, in black-toothed grimaces and howls. He got up—his every jostle of the double-bed mattress waking my mother—and went to the bathroom and peed (he would have said "urinated"). He threw on his tattered bathrobe and stepped along the hall and into the living room and turned on the light and read in his Bible. Even today I can envision him as I saw him so often, sitting and reading his Bible under a standing lamp. Verse after verse probably passed his lips chantlike, their meaning embedded in the type, not penetrating his thoughts. He must have put his index finger and middle finger on the words as he read them—he always did that— seeking to force some random passage into his mind. A fist hit the side of his jaw. Later he told me his head had nodded onto his own knuckles. He said he half-dreamed of men carrying pieces of boards and tree limbs as clubs coming in a swarm down the street. He had stood and faced them. He had gotten hit in the head. He had held out both arms and pushed the black children behind him. He'd have to take the first blows. His head snapped back upright. He said he must have dozed off again. Then he woke. He laid his Bible down and got up, went into the kitchen and drank a glass of water. The clock said three o'clock. Five more hours. He folded himself back into bed and pulled up the sheet. "Dorothy," he whispered, "rub my back. I can't sleep." She did for an hour, and listened. She always did that when he couldn't sleep. Later he reported that much to his surprise he "slept quite well that night." Perhaps he meant: "for the remainder of the night."

In the morning when he rolled over and put his feet on the floor, his eyes ached. He fell to his knees beside the bed as he always did every morning, folded his hands on the bedcovers, and tried to pray. As a small child wandering into my parents' bedroom in the early morning, I would find him like that. His loose pajamas hung all around him, concealing a torso still muscular at fifty-five, with taut wrestler's arms and legs, his feet dusted with the ever-present athlete's foot powder that also laid a blanket across the floor and lent a talcum scent to the bedroom. "Our father, not my will but thy will be done." He heard himself reciting the Lord's Prayer, line after line. And as each ritual set of words came, he strained to pull its meaning into full consciousness. He heard his inner voice mumbling, "For thine is the kingdom and the power and the glory forever. Amen." He clenched his fists, side-by-side on the bedspread, and squeezed his eyes tight in order to actually see the word *kingdom* as if written on a blackboard, then the word *power*, then the word *glory*.

He did not know what he was going to do. A man of action, he hated indecision. My brothers—David, Jonathan, and Paul—and my mother gathered around the breakfast table. I had left a year before for Europe, but I can see my family there just as when we were boys.

Everyone held hands. My father said a blessing. Then he read out loud the Twenty-third Psalm. When we were boys, every morning while we ate our oatmeal he sat in his pajamas and bathrobe and read the Bible to us before we went off to school, reading it straight through, Old Testament and then New Testament, explaining as he went: history, geography, ethical issues. My mother silently mouthed everything, word for word, so that my two deaf brothers could read her lips and understand what was being said. We knew the Bible better than anyone in town. But that morning he broke off the sequential reading and jumped to "The Lord is my shepherd, I shall not want." His voice cracked. "Even though I walk through the valley of the shadow of death, I fear no evil; for thou art with me." Then he ate his oatmeal.

Twenty-one-year-old David opened the dreaded subject: "Are you going over there to the school? Do you really intend to march through the mob?" My father heard himself say he did. "Well, I think you'll need a bodyguard. I'm going with you."

By that time David weighed in heavier than the rest of us, and at six foot one, he stood taller. Older by a year, I had won all of our fights up until his senior year in high school. Then David spurted up and out, and I didn't mess with him any more.

My father got up from the table, went into the bathroom to shave and give himself a sponge bath. He cleaned his nails and dressed in a summer suit and tie, tucking a fresh handkerchief into his left inside jacket pocket and, continuing his daily routine, half a dozen blank three-by-five cards into his right inside jacket pocket, for names and addresses of people new to him. He never left the house in anything less formal than a suit—often a three-piece—and tie. He felt a warmth in hearing that David wanted to accompany him, that their roles were switching, that the lead could be played by a son-protector as well as by a father-protector.

The two of them drove the Chevrolet over to Twelfth and Park, the meeting place designated by Daisy Bates two blocks from Central High. The hour approached eight. The group straggled together and milled about: Daisy Bates, my brother David, a local white minister (Colbert Cartwright),[1] two white ministers newly arrived as out-of-town observers (George A. Chauncey, First Presbyterian Church of Monticello, Arkansas, and Will D. Campbell from the National Council of Churches), two black ministers (Z. Z. Driver, and Harry Bass with no local pastoral affiliation), and a black lawyer (possibly C. C. Mercer). Joining that group were seven of the nine selected black students with an additional black girl (who after that day would change her mind about attempting to enroll in Central High). At 8:10 they would march. They all stood around silent, looking at each other.

Later my father described the scene: "I can't say the children looked afraid. The word I would use to describe them is *thoughtful*. They looked just like any eight boys and girls of high school age— fine, clean-cut youngsters.

"I felt a great compassion. I had an impulse to throw my arms around them and I thought: They're so much like the young people in my church, so much like the young people in my home, and I thought how I hated to see them go out there and face the mob.

"One of the Negro men came over to me and said, 'Well, Reverend Ogden, are you and these other ministers going with us?' And I said, 'Well, I don't know.' And he said, 'Well, you know at 8:10 we're going to start marching.' And everyone was silent.

"And I thought something should be said, being a minister, I guess. I didn't actually offer a prayer but I said, 'Now, young people, you are doing something this morning that takes a lot of faith and courage and I believe it is the right thing to do and I believe you are opening the way for many other young people to go to school to-gether. We don't know what that mob is going to try to do to you. Whether they're going to do anything, hurtful or not, we don't know. But we know it is a very bad situation. I want you to remember your own Martin Luther King and what he said about nonviolence. There was a man named Gandhi in India and he had the same idea and he helped to win the freedom of his people. Of course there was one whom we call Jesus Christ and it is written in the Scripture that when he was reviled he reviled not again.'

"And about this time, a Negro came over and he said, 'It's just about 8:09 now. Are you going with us or not?'

"I said, 'I don't know.'

"And he said, 'Reverend Ogden, isn't it about time you made up your mind?'

"And then, I can say it more in retrospect, this had the effect of making me feel that yes, I had to make up my mind whether I was going all the way from here on.

"And then I had a very strange feeling. And this is the kind of thing that we describe as something of a prophetic experience. I had the really strange feeling, as clear as day, and I felt: This is right; this is what I should do.

"There was not the slightest doubt but that I should do it. I ought to do it. And I felt this was the will of God for me. Every bit of fear just drained out."

"All right," my father said. "We will go with you."

In that moment he made a choice that would change his life and the course of history. He turned and began to walk down Park toward Central High. He did not look back. The little band followed along, two here and three there. My father led out. Then the black students and David. The two black pastors brought up the rear. The other white adults scattered into the crowd in order to observe. Daisy Bates stayed back so as not to stir up a riot. My father, David, and the black students moved in a group all alone. The other ministers, white and black, faded into the jostle. The marchers squeezed past the olive-brown trucks and half-tracks blocking the street at Central High. My father was leading eight black students (seven of the Nine plus Jane Hill) right into the guns of the military. He was putting at risk the lives of his own three boys and his wife. To endanger himself, to win sainthood through martyrdom for himself, he possessed that right. But did he have the right to bring down lethal retaliation on these boys and girls, to trigger the acid-throwing and drive-by shootings that he knew could maim and destroy children?

He walked. Inside him the turmoil had suddenly come to rest. His inner writhings through the night smoothed out. The acrid taste in his mouth dissipated. All at once with sharpest clarity he saw every soldier, every weapon, every helmet, the flying horse on a pump at the Magnolia Mobil gas station, each stone in the curb, the blades of grass that edged the sidewalk, every man and woman, for a millisecond each face frozen in the mob.

People down the street spotted the little group. They surged forward. They picked up their pace: heavy-necked burly men in short-sleeved shirts and hats; some younger with crew cuts and polo shirts; and hard-jawed, hair-sprayed, thick-armed women in dresses. Some of the guys laughed, smoked a cigarette, on a rowdy late-summer morning's adventure. Some pointed. "Look, there are the niggers. Get 'em."

My father kept going. It is a hard thing, he thought, to walk into a whole gang of hostile people. But this is what we've let ourselves in for. He glanced back. The eight, clutching their books, straggled along, with David, the two visiting white pastors, and the two local black pastors. Every three feet on the right they passed a soldier, rifle at the ready—hard-eyed, helmet low, back to the school, on guard. The mob force would confront them right at the front of the school.

A movement of soldiers shifted just behind the armed line. The line opened. Out stepped Lt. Col. Marion Johnson, commander of the troops, tan shirt with stars, a heavy helmet hooding his eyes, middle-aged, beginning double chin, a mouth set for giving orders, a thick white nightstick in his grip. He stuck the baton at Carlotta Walls's stomach, at Ernest Green's chest. An aide, rifle up, stood beside him. David over to his left. My father stopped. The group collected in front of Lt. Col. Johnson. The mob closed in a half-circle behind the children. Silence.

"Are you here to see to it that these children enter this school or to prevent them from entering?" My father spoke in his resonant pulpit voice, shaping the kind of formal formulation he used in public. He wanted all to hear. He wanted witnesses. He wanted no ambiguity. Under the protection of the National Guard he felt relief for the children and safe from the angry rabble pressing in behind them.

"The school is off-limits to these people," said Lt. Col. Johnson, shoving his nightstick toward Carlotta Walls and Ernest Green and Gloria Ray in front.

"Does that mean that these children cannot be admitted to school?"

"Yes. That is what it means."[2]

One of the black leaders stepped in: "We understood from Governor Faubus that the soldiers are here to keep the peace, for law and order."

"During the night my orders were changed by the governor," said Lt. Col. Johnson.

And then something happened that my father said he never understood. Lt. Col. Johnson and his aide turned on their heels and marched back to the safety of the campus, the line of soldiers opening for them and then shutting, leaving the young black intruders at the mercy of hundreds of hostile white people. "The silence was so thick," my father said, "you could cut it with a knife.

"This young Negro leader came up to me and said, 'We'll take them home,' and then he looked at me as though to say: Now it's your job. And I thought, I brought them in and now what am I going to do?

"I thought there must be some way; there's just got to be some way. But how do you get through hundreds of people who are all around you? Hundreds of them, just standing there, looking at you. How do you get out of there?

"And then I saw four men with cameras and I presumed they were newspaper photographers. And on impulse, more than anything else, I turned to them.

"I said, 'Gentlemen, I'm sure you realize the time has come for these young people to go back to their cars and return to their homes. And I'm going to ask you, please, to make a way for them.'

"They started backing up, heel on toe, these four men and the mob back of them, which was much more important. As they backed, a little narrow path opened up.

"I said, 'Go on,' and the children started walking single file, all our little party, and we just kept on going and I came out last of all. I was afraid to look back because, you know, I thought if I looked back it might provoke the mob.

"So I just kept going, going, going, and I never looked back and we were not followed and were not molested. We got the children in the cars and Mrs. Bates took them at once to the school board. I did not go with them. I returned to my home.

"The next days the reaction in my church and among my fellow ministers was not friendly. At first, my associates seemed more puzzled than angry. 'Why did you do it?' a fellow pastor asked me."[3]

The day before a young black lawyer, C. C. Mercer, had come to my father's church study. He told my father: "Our Negro people are gathered in little groups in their homes in this city with the shades drawn. And they are weeping and praying. For them this is like a birthday with no birthday present, like Christmas with no Christmas tree. You see, Negroes have been waiting for this day for a long time. This was to be the beginning of their educational freedom. More than two hundred Negro boys and girls were eligible to go to Central High. Now it's only nine, and even that little group has an angry mob out in the street. Mr. Ogden, you can't imagine what a tragic thing this is in the hearts and minds and lives of our Negro people."

Elizabeth Eckford, age fifteen, got caught in the street. Every black girl feared isolation in the street more than anything else—the sheer terror of being caught out alone. The threat of rape was everywhere. White males did it and black girls didn't talk. Since earliest slave days, rape of black girls by white owners characterized male-female

(Opposite): The *Arkansas Democrat,* front page, September 4, 1957.

Home Edition

ARKANSAS DEMOCRAT

Today's News Today

EIGHTY-SIXTH YEAR—No. 338   Entered as Second Class Matter, Post Office, Little Rock, Ark.   LITTLE ROCK, WEDNESDAY EVENING, SEPTEMBER 4, 1957   24 PAGES   PRICE 5¢

GOVERNOR FAUBUS ORDERS—Lt. Col. Marion Johnson, commander of National Guard troops, turns back group of Negroes seeking to enter Central High School today. He said he was acting on orders of Governor Faubus not to admit Negroes. The Negroes left peaceably. (Democrat Photo by Counts.)

Armed Troops Turn Back 9 Negroes At Central High School

(By GEORGE DOUTHIT.)
Democrat Staff Writer.

Nine Negro students attempting to integrate into Little Rock Central High School today were turned back by National Guardsmen "on orders of Governor Faubus."

There were no incidents except for some catcalls as a crowd followed a lone Negro girl who walked the length of the front of the school in advance of the main group of seven which was halted some minutes later.

The governor, who ordered troops around the high school Sunday night, denied yesterday he was blocking integration as ordered by the federal courts and contended he was only maintaining "law and order" in the face of threatened violence.

Today, Negro leaders accompanying seven of the students asked a National Guard officer if he were preventing their entering the school on the orders of the governor. The officer replied: That is right.

The Negroes, delayed only for names and photographs by a squad of photographers and reporters, retraced their steps. They were allowed to give their names but when asked out of state newsman asked: What do you think of all of this?" an unidentified white man told the Negroes to keep quiet. It appeared to be accompanying them.

The group of seven Negroes assembled at 10th and Park marched in a group to the school corner at 14th and Park. They were led by a middle-aged Negro who R.A. [illegible]

At their approach the curb lined with armed Guardsmen, the group was pushed back, they then stepped into the street and were confronted by the Guard officer, Lt. Col. Marion Johnson, commanding the troops.

Harry Bass, Little Rock Negro leader, asked the colonel if h

(Other pictures on pages 2 and 5.)

were preventing them from entering the school. The colonel said that was right.

Bass then asked: "I just want to get this straight. You are doing this on the orders of the governor, is that correct?"

Colonel Johnson said: "That is right."

Bass replied: "All right. We do not want to disobey any orders of the state militia."

By this time, the reporters and photographers who had been notified along the block in front of the school gathered around the group and began asking names and questions for themselves.

The students, five girls and two boys in this group, gave their names as follows: Carlotta Walls, 16, Gloria Ray, 14, Jane Hill, 15, Ernest Green, 15, Thelma Jean Mothershed, 16, Minnie Jean Brown, 16, and Jefferson Thomas, 15.

All said they were coming to Little Rock Central from Horace Mann High School, an all-Negro school. They said

See TROOPS on page 2.

Faubus Says Guard Told To Stop Negroes

By R. B. MAYFIELD.
Democrat Staff Writer.

Governor Faubus confirmed at a press conference today he had issued orders to Arkansas National Guardsmen not to permit Negro students to enter Little Rock Central High School. He said the order was issued to Adj. Gen. Sherman T. Clinger about 11:30 p. m. yesterday. He told newsmen he did not consider this order a violation of the federal court order to integrate the school.

Governor Faubus said the order was issued to maintain peace and order and that he issued it as the chief executive of the state whose responsibility it is to keep the peace.

For the second straight morning his office was jammed for the press conference as additional agencies from over the country sent their representatives to cover this momentous problem of desegregation in face of federal court orders.

The first question was whether the Negro students were turned back on his orders.

He said: "That is correct. I sent an order to Col. [illegible] Clinger who issued them to Colonel Johnson in charge of the at the school."

He said the orders were given directly to General Clinger. He said the orders were given from the field. This is the place [illegible]

"You are directed to place any of his office was assembled these schools for colored students and to place off limits to white students those persons heretofore operated and exclusively set up for white students. This order will remain in effect until desegregation of the Guard or until further orders."

He was asked what prompted him to issue these new orders to Negro students as opposed to Little's view of the advance said that the Guardsmen were instructed only to maintain law and order.

The three students identified themselves as Carlotta Walls, Jane Hill and Jefferson Thomas.

Bass told a Democrat reporter that the object of the visit was to "work advice on what to do next now that the students had been turned away from the school."

The colonel said the three

See U. S. on page 2.

District Attorney Checks Case

Possible Violation Of Court Order Being Probed

By MARGARET FRICK.
Democrat Staff Writer.

The U. S. attorney launched an investigation today to determine whether the federal court order was violated when Guardsmen acting on Governor Faubus' orders refused to admit Negro students to Central High School.

U. S. Attorney Osro Cobb said the following statement:

"Through and factual investigation will be made as to any and all interference with the order of the federal court.

Shortly after this, three Negro students accompanied by Little's office but the attorney said they were released and they were "maintaining."

The three students identified themselves as Carlotta Walls, Jane Hill and Jefferson Thomas, was his FBO interceptor crashed just north of Perrin Air Force Base.

Bass said a Democrat reporter that the object of the visit was to "work advice on what to do next now that the students had been turned away from the school."

The colonel said the three

See U. S. on page 2.

He Was Right

Reno, Nev. [AP]—Oldtimer Wayne Hinckley figured that if he posted the combination on the outside of his safe, would-be thieves wouldn't bother to damage the safe. He was right. Burglars used the combination, got at a $256 in cash and $2,581 in checks.

Integration Order Covers All 3 Schools

By BOBBIE FORSTER.
Democrat Staff Writer.

All "senior high schools" in the Little Rock school district are under federal court order to integrate classes "forthwith," and National Guardsmen were posted at Central High school this morning.

The all inclusive order handed down in an exact four-minute hearing by Federal Judge Ronald N. Davies last night applied equally to Central, Hall and Horace Mann High Schools.

A three line statement issued by the Little Rock Board of Education after a one hour closed door session last night also applies to all three high schools equally.

School authorities have maintain that they did not expect any Negro students to enroll at Hall, although they have said there are a "few" eligible ones live in that area. No white students have been expected to enroll in the Horace Mann, formerly all-Negro school, but if any live in that area are otherwise eligible they could not be refused admittance under the court order.

Judge Davies called last night's hearing after school board action forced a petition that the school board not be held in contempt of a federal court order to begin graduated integration this semester.

The pleading was filed after the board had asked Negroes be admitted to Central or any other white high school yesterday because of Governor Faubus' statements on Sunday.

The school board will do whatever you say in fitting and proper under the circumstances," declared attorney A. F. House said last night.

Mr. House insisted that the school board not be held in contempt. Mr. House maintained he had no interest from the plan of this action, but that a "combination of events in Central or any other white high school yesterday."

Solon Calls For Curbs On Credit

Would Revive Controls Over Installment Buying

Washington [P]—Senator O'Mahoney [D], Wyo.] proposed today that installment buying controls be revived as an antidote to inflation.

O'Mahoney, a member of the Senate-House Economic Committee, said in an interview he agrees with President Eisenhower that inflation is the nation's major internal problem at this time. But Mr. Wyoming senator said he doubts it can be controlled on an entirely voluntary basis.

"Installment buying has reached an all-time peak," he said. "Our people are mortgaging their futures for things they can't pay for now and some controls are needed for this situation. Regulation W, under which the Federal Reserve System could put a brake on this buying, ought to be revived."

Under that wartime regulation, both minimum down payments and maximum payment periods were prescribed for automobiles, appliances and other items. Authority he it has expired.

Elsewhere told his seven-man Advance yesterday that he can not advocating a buyers' strike but did believe Americans should buy as selectively and carefully. He said he thinks legislation should curb the long rate are and detaining. He said the actions of the Treasury Federal Reserve Board and other agencies are all directed toward combatting price rises.

The Weather

Little Rock, North Little Rock, and Vicinity — Partly cloudy this afternoon, tonight and Thursday with little change in temperature. High this afternoon in the low 90's. Low tonight near 70.

Arkansas — Partly cloudy this afternoon, tonight and Thursday with a few isolated thundershowers in south portion this afternoon. Not much change in the temperature. High this afternoon, and 90's by low 90's; low tonight, in the 60's.

Extended Forecast — Wednesday p. m. to Monday p. m.—Temperatures will average one to 3 degrees below normal in northeast Arkansas and near normal elsewhere with minor daily changes. Precipitation moderate to locally heavy in scattered thundershowers occurring mainly before Sunday.

8 a. m. 70   6 p. m. 81
7 a. m. 72   10 p. m. 84
6 a. m. 75   11 p. m. 87

Maximum yesterday 90
Minimum yesterday 70
Sunset today .... 6:32 p. m.
Sunrise tomorrow .... 5:46 p. m.
Precipitation 24 hours to 1 a. m. today .... None
Precipitation since Jan. 1, 1957 .... plus 15.82 in.
Departure from normal since Jan. 1, 1957 .... plus 15.82 in.

FIRST TO ARRIVE—The first Negro student to arrive at Little Rock Central High today was Elizabeth Echford, 15.

(1) She walks toward the National Guardsmen on her way to school.

(2) The Guardsman points toward 14th and tells her she cannot enter the line and to school.

(3) She walks on toward 14th down Park before the line of guards followed by an angry crowd and stopped at a bus stop bench. (Democrat Photos by Will Counts.)

Washington Silent On Developments

By JACK CLELLAND.
Democrat Washington Bureau.

Washington — Officials at the Justice Department here today maintained a "no comment" attitude on the day's developments in Little Rock.

All they would say is that the department is studying the situation as it was directed to do yesterday by President Eisenhower.

Problems Too Numerous To Talk About

Integration problems in Little Rock schools forced cancellation of a talk today by Supt. Virgil Blossom.

He was scheduled to have addressed the Downtown Lions Club luncheon on "Problems of Our Public Schools Today."

Three Safe After Jets Collide

Dover, Del. [P]—Two twin-engine F86 Scorpion jet fighter planes crashed over Delaware bay today. The Air Force said one man was missing and three parachuted to safety.

Capt. James Bouchard, public information officers of Dover Air Force Base, said the collision occurred shortly after take off about one mile off Pickering Beach.

Bouchard said three crewmen parachuted to safety and the fourth was missing. Identification were withheld until it could be determined which man was missing.

The planes, each of which carried a pilot and radar observer from the 96th Fighter Interceptor Squadron of the CBS Air Defense Wing at Dover AFB.

Tennessee Flier Killed in Crash

Sherman, Tex. [P]—First Lt. William R. Simpson, 23, Dyersburg, Tenn. was killed last night when his F86D interceptor crashed just north of Perrin Air Force Base.

Base officials said Simpson was on a routine training flight and had entered the landing pattern when he crashed. The cause was not immediately determined.

He is survived by his wife, Patricia Leah Simpson, Sherman.

Crowd Jeers as Negro Students Attempt to Enter Central High

By ROBERT TROUT.
Democrat Staff Writer.

A 15-year-old Negro girl approached the National Guard line of resistance at 14th and Park at 7:55 a. m. today, attempting to gain entry to Little Rock Central High School, but was refused passageway through the line of armed soldiers.

Elizabeth Echford, wearing sun glasses and dressed in white trim with a checkered black trim tore to her skirt and carrying a small green notebook, then calmly walked the length of Park in 14th and sat on a bus stop bench while a crowd of some 150 whites formed a circle around her and jeered. There was no violence.

As she walked along the Guard line in the street in front of the high school the crowd followed, calling her names and some said, "Go home nigger, you never got into this school. We don't want you here."

She sat straight ahead as she hit the crowd to the bus stop where she halted. But at first refused to give her name or any other information to anyone, but later told newsmen her name and age after a second Negro youth walked over to her when he too failed to pass through the line of armed men.

Soon after the girl alighted on the bench and the crowd moved back up the street to the Guard line at the school, a second Negro student walked up Park toward 10th and stopped before a group of

Guardsmen brandishing rifles. They told him he could not pass.

The student was wearing a checkered sport shirt, dark trousers and was carrying a small black spiral notepad. He gave his name as Terrance Roberts, 15, 2301 Howard. He talked freely to reporters.

See JEERS on page 5.

Terrance, the son of a kitchen worker at Veterans Hospital in North Little Rock, told the Democrat that he had been to several morning meetings recently with three Negro students who were called to gather with their parents by the school superintendent and other

CAT CALLS—Elizabeth Eckford, 15, the first Negro student to attempt entry to Little Rock Central High today, walks down Park followed by a crowd of some 250 shouting whites. (Democrat Photo.)

Lloyd, Yugoslav Chief to Confer

London [P]—British Foreign Secretary Selwyn Lloyd left for Yugoslavia today on a mission to counter recent Russian attempts to woo President Tito.

"I hope to have discussions in the international problems of the day," Lloyd said before leaving London airport aboard an RAF jet liner.

Two Russian Ships Sail English Channel

Dover, England [P]—Two Russian ships—presumably a Yugoslavia-bound cruiser and destroyer — steamed westward through the English Channel today. Admiralty lookouts reported the movement of the vessels, saying there were about four miles off Dover.

The Russians announced this week that a cruiser and a mine-laying destroyer were en route to Yugoslavia on a goodwill visit.

Auto Traffic Scoreboard
Death Toll

To Date:	1957	1956
Little Rock	6	7
N. Little Rock ...	3	4
Pulaski Co.	26	23
Arkansas	123	293
1956 Total for Little Rock		17
1956 Total for N. L. Rock		8
1956 Total for Pulaski Co.		36
1956 Total for Arkansas		407

Bomb Kills Woman

Havana [P]—A bomb exploded last night in the ladies room of a movie theater, killing a 25-year-old woman.

relations in the Old South. In *Long Shadow*, Daisy Bates writes that her mother had been raped and killed by white men.

Because Elizabeth's family did not have a telephone, during the night of September 3 Daisy Bates had failed to reach her with the information about the morning's meeting place for the Nine. Elizabeth had made a dress especially for school opening. She had ironed it that night. The next morning she got off the city bus wearing her new dress and the special sunglasses she had saved for, and headed for the front entrance of Central High. The milling crowd began to move in behind her. A few steps ahead, she crossed the street to walk along safely behind the National Guard line.

But instead of providing protection, the soldiers stood in her way and forced her back into the street toward the crowd. "Here she comes. Get ready. We'll get the nigger bitch." Elizabeth clutched her books to her chest. She held her head high. She felt no terror. But suddenly her knees shook horribly. Could she make it to the center entrance? Later she said, "It was the longest block I ever walked in my whole life." Still, if she had trouble, she thought, the guards would protect her.

At the center of the line Elizabeth walked up to a Guard. He stared straight ahead. She could not pass. Farther on she saw the path that led over to the school building. The cursing and name-calling behind her had numbed her. Guards let several white students through. Elizabeth followed. They snapped back into position, one shoving a bayonet in her face. Others moved to the assistance of their comrade, they too raising their bayonets to ward off the threat of the black teenage girl.

Elizabeth turned. The crowd pressed in. She searched for a gentle face, any sign of help. An older woman caught her attention. Perhaps some kindness resided there. Elizabeth stepped toward her. The woman spat on Elizabeth. She turned back. The bayonets pointed a lethal fence.

Down the street she spotted a bench at a bus stop she knew well. She thought, "If I can only get there, I will be safe." She walked. The mob followed, shouting. Elizabeth kept saying to herself, "If I can only get there, I will be safe. If I can only get there. . . ." A kind of mantra to block out the sound and the horror.

Stepping in behind her, right on her heels, came Sammie Dean Parker. Books on her arm, in a fresh dark dress with light buttons, light scarf, neat haircut, cute, ready for her second day at school, cursing, egging her friend Hazel Bryan to join in shouts of "nigger bitch." A photograph of Hazel's wrenched mouth and squinted eyes in that moment became the face of racial hate in newspapers and magazines all over the world. At school Sammie Dean would go after Elizabeth with a fury.

Elizabeth reached the bench, at Sixteenth and Park, and her knees gave way. She sat. Its familiarity gave her comfort. She got up and crossed the street to a store to call a cab, but the people in the store would not let her in. She went back to the bench. The crowd was waiting: "We got us one. Drag her over to this tree. Get a rope."

Terrence Roberts appeared. He was the other member of the Nine who had missed the meeting place—because he lived on the opposite side of Central High and was arriving from that direction. He said, "Come on, let's walk together. I'll go with you. I'll walk you home."

"Uh-uh. No," Elizabeth told him. "In a crowd I'll be safer." If the two of them got isolated, they wouldn't escape alive. The bus would come. She rode it a lot. Terrence Roberts left.

L. C. Bates, Daisy Bates's husband, came and sat beside her. "He showed me how he had a pistol in his pants. I *did not want* a gun there. *That* scared me." She waved him away.

All at once a middle-aged white woman emerged from the throng and planted herself on the bench and put her arm around Elizabeth. Mrs. Grace Lorch turned to the bystanders. "Leave this child alone," she started shouting. "Why are you tormenting this child? Six months from now you'll hang your heads in shame."

"She ranted and raved," said Elizabeth. "That terrified me because all at once the crowd—sort of milling around—got angrier and angrier. They howled. She wouldn't stop."

"All of you treating a young girl like that. You all just get out of here. You should be ashamed of yourselves. I'd be proud to have my daughter go to school with this Negro child."

Elizabeth said, "That *really* got the crowd angry. Now I was really terrified. I wanted Mrs. Lorch out of there in the worst way. Mrs. Lorch brought trouble with her." The crowd quieted down. Elizabeth froze inside. In her imagination she could feel the roughness of a loop of heavy rope around her neck. But somehow instead of lunging at her, people began turning away and heading off down to the far end of the street. Elizabeth did not know it, but they had sighted my father and the group of black students approaching the school from the other direction. The mob started abandoning her to go after larger prey.

The city bus rolled up. Elizabeth climbed aboard.

On its front page that week the Bateses' paper, the *Arkansas State Press*, printed two photographs from the morning's events. One showed the National Guard commander turning away the black children, with my father; the other showed Elizabeth Eckford, already turned away and walking with a jeering mob behind her, a white man in a bow tie beside her. It was Benjamin Fine of the *New York Times*, telling her, "Don't let them see you cry."

Elizabeth Eckford became the most famous girl in the world. A young stringer for the *Arkansas Gazette* named Will Counts had gone over to Central High that morning to shoot some pictures for a Sunday magazine story. Regular news photographers all carried the Speed Graphic, a big, square, clumsy box with a flash unit the size of a saucer and a lamp as big as a household light bulb. It produced four-by-five-inch negatives. It took its handler five to ten seconds to shoot, pull out the frame with the film, reverse the frame, and push it back in and shoot again. The camera identified a man as a reporter from five hundred feet away. In addition, all official reporters wore dress shirts. Counts, on the other hand, wore a plaid shirt and jeans and packed a small 35 mm Leica, so he could palm it and disappear into a crowd. More important, when he raised it to his eye, he could fire off frames as fast as he could advance the film and press the button.

Will Counts with his Leica caught all the action around Elizabeth that morning. One particular photo that went out on the wire was picked up immediately by newspapers and magazines throughout the United States and Europe and Asia. There Elizabeth steps forward, everybody's young first-day high school girl: head high, poised, dark-skinned, fine mouth slightly pursed, gold-dot earrings, sunglasses, looking straight ahead and slightly downward, holding a book and a loose-leaf binder in her left arm against her chest, in a freshly ironed, light-colored shirtwaist with pleated, flared skirt, new white buck loafers, and bobby socks. The viewer's eye shifts from Elizabeth to the white high school girl at her heels, Hazel Bryan. Hazel too wears a freshly ironed dress, has short, black hair. She's white. Her face twists in an angry jeer. Her mouth opens full, lips

Elizabeth Eckford, one of the Nine, taunted by the mob outside Central High, September 4, 1957. (Photograph by Will Counts.)

jutting out, baring her teeth. Her eyes squeeze tight, a furrow up the middle of her forehead. Her fists clench. She curses into the back of Elizabeth's head, screaming behind her. Beside Hazel walks Sammie Dean Parker: petite, stylish dark dress with light buttons, a scarf on the front, also books on her arm, slightly bobbed hair, pert. She eggs her friend Hazel on.

Elizabeth walks hemmed in on three sides by the crowd, all white. To her left, a heavy-set, hard-jawed, middle-aged woman in a dress, another bullet-eyed, middle-aged woman beside her. Following Hazel, two high-school-aged boys in short-sleeved shirts, one with a crew cut, laughing together. Behind Sammie Dean a stout, middle-aged man, stomach bulging at his belt, open-necked, short-sleeved shirt and hat, mouth set, stepping forward and staring intently at Elizabeth's back—Sammie Dean's father.

That scene caught the imagination of people everywhere: a shy, young, demure, dark-skinned girl going for an education jammed in by a white mob out to stop her. People wrote to her from all over the world: Australia, Japan, Liberia, Mexico, New Zealand, Spain, Sweden, the United Kingdom, and West Germany, where I was teaching classes in a German high school. The picture has been reproduced thousands of times. To this day it stands as the signature photograph in the struggle for racial equality.

Hazel's features instantly became the international face of hate. She would have to live with that image of herself for the rest of her life. During the first week of school, Hazel would pull out of Central High to attend a segregated high school. Inside Central High, Sammie Dean would become the female leader of Elizabeth's torturers. It would take forty years before Elizabeth could bring herself to talk about what went on.

How had Elizabeth Eckford prepared herself for the coming ordeal? Her mother recalled, "The night before Elizabeth went to school I told her to be sure and read her Bible that night and again in the morning before she started out." Elizabeth herself said, "I read the Fourth Psalm the night before and the Twenty-seventh Psalm that morning before I caught the bus."[4]

Psalm 4 concludes:

In peace I will both lie down and sleep;
For thou alone, O Lord, makest me dwell in safety.

And Psalm 27 opens:

The Lord is my light and my salvation; whom shall I fear?
The Lord is the stronghold of my life; of whom shall I be afraid?

Religion and the church played a major role in the life of each of the Little Rock Nine. So did family. Without exception all had strong relationships with their parents, and each family participated actively in the life of a church. Of the Nine, Ernest Green and Melba Pattillo were the only ones who did not have a father who lived in their home and was employed outside the home: Green's mother was widowed and Pattillo's mother was divorced. Minnijean Brown, Elizabeth Eckford, Ernest Green, Melba Pattillo, and Gloria Ray were members of African Methodist Episcopal churches. Carlotta Walls and her family were Methodists. Jefferson Thomas was Baptist. Thelma Mothershed and her family were members of the Mt. Sinai Christian Church, and Terrence Roberts's family belonged to the Seventh-day Adventist church. It was Minnijean Brown's pastor, Z. Z. Driver, who had walked with the children on that fateful Integration Wednesday. The Reverend Rufus King Young, the pastor of Ernest Green, Melba Pattillo, and Gloria Ray—at the Bethel AME Church—would soon emerge as an increasingly powerful church voice for integration.

After breakfast the next morning my father brought the brightest-eyed visitor over to the school to see what was happening: my little eight-year-old brother, Paul. He had spotted his father on television last night, and now he wanted to go over to Central High so he could be on television. The Nine had stayed home. Most students sat in their classrooms. Soldiers lined the periphery of the grounds. My father and Paul walked around and examined the jeeps and the half-tracks and stacked rifles. They went up and nodded to soldiers in their boots and helmets. My father explained yesterday's events to his deaf son, pacing the distances, pointing, laying out the scene in minutest detail: "We were coming along here. The mob started closing in on us from just over there." Paul stared at my father's mouth and hands as intently as he stared at the armed camp around them. Paul was totally deaf. In a few days he would return to his school in St. Louis, where he was learning to read lips and to speak. My parents let nothing escape him.

My father could reach his deaf son, but could he reach his congregation? The furor in the streets altered his thirty-year-old way of preaching. In the months to follow he discarded many sermon-writing habits he had practiced since his seminary days. Step by step he developed a new approach, a new style, a new emphasis, and a new voice. This process of change evolved with him as much unconsciously as consciously.

When my father preached, he positioned himself erect behind the lectern, hardly moving. In his Little Rock church he would take his place on a pulpit platform raised some four feet above the floor and look out over a semicircle of pews that rose slightly toward the rear of the sanctuary. He stood about five foot eight inches, not a tall man but firm with a solid chest and muscular arms. Except for his black robe, he refused the further adornments of a turned collar, white tabs beneath his chin, or a gold or wooden cross around his neck. At fifty-five, his hair still grew thick and black, somewhat wavy. Now when I am seventy, I can still see him each morning as he brushed it back, counting one hundred strokes. He had the square jaw, full lips, brown eyes, Roman nose, and slightly swarthy look of what his mother—a Mississippi blue blood—had always referred to as "our Spanish ancestor." (My father's mother traced her ancestry person-for-person all the way back to the Mayflower, as did his father, but she would subside into uncharacteristic vagueness when it came to further information about this alleged Mediterranean forebear.) My father did not wear glasses. He spoke in the round, measured tones of a former debate-team leader. He knew how to support his voice from his abdomen, like an actor. He did not gesture, save occasionally to punctuate a point with the up-and-down motion of his left arm from the elbow, his index finger extended. He often kept the index finger of his right hand at his place in his sermon notes.

He wrote out his sermon notes in full, phrasing each key point meticulously. He composed his Sunday messages in ink, on both back and front of eight-and-a-half-by-eleven-inch sheets cut in half, his notes filling from eight to a dozen of these half sheets. He did not read a sermon. Rather, he spoke it, glancing at his notes. Often he laid out a sermon at least twice as long as his regular twenty minutes. He would preach half of it on the given Sunday and save the other half for a later Sunday.

Normally my father constructed a sermon around a detailed exegesis of the biblical passage that he had selected for his text. He possessed a scholar's instincts, and he still retained some command of Hebrew and Greek from his college and seminary days. Often he would read to his people both the King James translation of his selected text and the Revised Standard Version. He loved to work through the identification of biblical place names, to explain relevant history, to list synonyms and cognates, and to cite biblical analogues and parallel passages. Sometimes he did not get to the burden of his message until the very last page or two of his sermon.

He would highlight key words for explanation, discover connotations and shades of meaning, and build a historical framework from personal names and place names. He always relished a neat turn of phrase, a clever pun, a bon mot. Assonance, alliteration, and the ironic juxtaposition of images mark such sermon titles as "Christ in Crisis," "Peace and Palm Branches," "The Sword and the Star."

He made up witty sayings, and he collected aphorisms, wordplays, maxims.

"A text out of context is a pretext." He elaborated on that one Sunday, referring to some conservative church leaders who held that the Bible promoted racial discrimination. Halfway through a sermon he would begin introducing illustrations, often from local newspaper clippings pinned to the sheets. Each message included at least one serious story from which he would draw a thought or a moral. And usually one funny story. One Sunday when the congregation was about to discuss the annual budget, he told his flock: "Some pastors are said to shear their sheep before they feed them."

He enjoyed nothing more than reading aloud powerful and poetic passages from the Psalms, the Old Testament prophets, from Jesus's teachings and the Apostle Paul's letters. He counted it a scandal if a minister entered the pulpit and stumbled through the Scripture reading. He never failed to rehearse the morning's Bible passages out loud, often marking with a pencil his pauses, emphases, and correct pronunciations. Whenever he preached as a guest in someone else's pulpit, he invariably asked to be permitted also to read aloud the Bible passages that came early in the service—ordinarily read by the host pastor—"in order to try out my voice." He was also testing the acoustics while becoming comfortable with the different congregation. He left nothing to improvisation if he could help it, always rehearsing a baptismal rite with the parents before performing it and, for a marriage ceremony, always walking through even the most minute moves with the couple, parents, and wedding party, and practicing the lines with them.

Pride also governed my father's attitudes and his actions.

He always wore a full suit, sometimes a three-piece. He did not own a sport jacket. He almost never bought new clothes. Every Saturday night he shined his shoes, high-top and of especially soft leather because of fallen arches and incurable athlete's foot. He kept his nails immaculate—he had a particular way of holding a pair of scissors (he always had a favorite pair) reversed in his left hand so that he could trim the nails on his right hand—and always kept a fresh-daily white pocket handkerchief inside his suit-jacket pocket.

He chose his words as carefully as he chose his attire. He kept his facts as meticulously accurate as the names and family relationships of his parishioners. He never said anything that he did not know to be true—without a qualifier. His command of the Bible was legendary among his colleagues, as was at this time his command of the literature and printed news of racial matters. All his life his friends marveled at his exhaustive recall of facts and names.

He stood always with shoulders squared, wishing he were a taller man and always, even at the end of his life, reminding me "to stand up straight although your somewhat academic posture [he meant *slouch*] is quite pleasant." He had been a wrestler in college, had given wrestling exhibitions with a fellow student trained in Japan in wrestling, and had played volleyball in his forties down at the YMCA. He enjoyed using the word "trim" to describe physically fit people, including himself. Even until the time his first grandchild, my daughter, came along, he would take us all to a swimming pool and then climb up to the high diving board, do a handstand on its very end, and drop into the water in a graceful head-first dive. Women found him handsome and had apparently done so since his youth, though he seemed to have been largely unaware of it. With the college wrestler's physique came a pair of strong hands. He often showed me how the end joint on the little finger of his right hand remained permanently bent from a volleyball injury.

In his personal relationships, he was a man of old-fashioned dignity and courtesy. At the dinner table he always stood behind my mother's chair and slipped it under her as she sat. He did the same for any woman guest at our table. We never touched our food until one of us or a guest—or he himself—had said the blessing and my mother had taken the first bite.

Even when there were guests—which was the case almost every other night—he was always at pains to bring us children into the dinner conversation, sometimes priming each of us in private with a joke that we could then tell at the table. My mother often said that she fell in love with him "because he was so affectionate." The word was that she had accepted his marriage proposal after turning down two other young men.

Careful thought, clear headedness, and wide-ranging reference to places and people characterized his appearances in the pulpit, rather than the force of persuasive oratory and charisma. It was not for naught that he had majored in history in college. Undertones of admonition, moralizing, even reproach sometimes lurked beneath the surfaces of his serious conversation, public and private. He had ingested those forms and feelings from earliest childhood. His mother spoke that way. Sometimes he spoke that way, often unwillingly and unknowingly, and when he did, it did not endear him to others. But the undercurrent of reproach vanished at home when he talked from the heart, and when he went walking in the woods, and when at the church he conducted his regular Wednesday evening Bible study, and when he visited with people much below him in social advantage, with those downtrodden and in need of help or solace. He felt at ease with country people and blacks, not with middle-class businessmen or urban clergy of his own status and educational level. He dealt more comfortably with women than with men. He possessed more the gift of reasoning than the knack for persuading, more the facts of a physician than the twinkle of a beloved teacher.

In the next Sunday's church bulletin, September 8, my father printed as his sermon title, "With Liberty and Justice for All: The Danger of Rejecting Jesus." Would he talk to his congregation about the black students, about the racial issue, about his act of defiance, about his motivations? He had done it without the least congregational consensus and he knew it. Would he try to persuade them? Could he carry his people along with him, or would he alienate them? Could he bring himself to mention the specifics of social and political crisis from his pulpit? Ironically, on that very Sunday morning, along with delivering a sermon he was also to welcome publicly Central Presbyterian's missionary to Africa, Emily Boehler, home on furlough from Kakinda, in the Congo.

From his earliest pastorates, my father had always put on his ministerial robe in order to preach the Word of God. Outwardly Presbyterian ministers denied the special sanctity of their place in the pulpit, but inwardly they knew and cherished it. On that morning of September 8, my father took up the story of Jesus's expulsion from his boyhood home in Nazareth. Jesus had returned for a visit. There in the Nazareth synagogue Jesus read aloud from the prophet Isaiah: "The Lord has sent me . . . to set at liberty those who are oppressed." Jesus's kinsmen and former neighbors became so upset at his teaching that they ran him out of town. From my father's sermon notes it is clear that he found his own situation perilously close to that of Jesus. Yet he did not say it outright. In the church service bulletin he referred only tangentially to the integration crisis: "Let us pray ear-

nestly regarding all matters in the life of our community and state."
He would preach the same sermon as a guest in Oakland, California,
the following spring, and he would add, "All the Southern Presbyterian ministers whom I know in Little Rock occupy approximately
the same position as your pastor [i.e., pro-school integration], except
one." The "one" soon played an ominous role in my father's life.

Over in front of Central High that Sunday afternoon he met with
Frank McGee of NBC television news. McGee had asked him to select
and bring along a dozen white Central High students for an interview program about the turmoil. Someone else had gathered a dozen
against integration. McGee knew my father would choose students
for it, and he had. From the outset the media had recognized my father as a go-to man. So did the hate mongers.

In his pulpit during the month of September, my father fas-
tened on the epistle of 1 John. He held to it for most of that fall. In
his notes for September 15, he experimented with a variety of sermon titles such as "The Greatest Love Letter," "The Way of Love
and Grace," "The Way of Light and Love," "The Law of Love," and
"The Way of Life Beyond 'Law.' " Finally he fixed on the title "Beyond the Law." He said, "The major ideas in 1 John are overlapping,
interwoven, blended. Like the interests of Little Rock and Arkansas
and the U.S.A." He also sorted out major contrasts that he found in
John's letter: "between light and darkness, love and hate, obedience
and disobedience, sin and righteousness." John the epistle writer
was composing a hortatory letter to a Christian congregation. John
encouraged them: "I write this to you who believe . . . that you may
know that you have eternal life." And John admonished them: "He
who hates his brother is in the darkness and walks in the darkness,
and does not know where he is going." With a special vigor my father
read out John's lines from the church lectern, proclaiming a particular sentence that became a headline in his own philosophy: "He who
does the will of God abides for ever."

In the same way, he sought helpful biblical passages for his own
inner life. In his introduction to 1 John he told his congregation,
"John is a book of *confidence* and *assurance* and *certainty*" (my father's
emphasis). When a fortnight earlier he had made the decision to go
out with the black students and face the mob, he himself needed
the confidence, assurance, and certainty that he was doing the right
thing.

On one page of his sermon notes my father wrote, "There are people in our community who are very much *exercised* over the actions of some officials whom they feel have gone 'beyond the law of this nation'—in the sense that they have made the law of the state paramount to that of the country as a whole." He was talking about Governor Faubus's calling out the National Guard.

Black Pastors

On the calling out of the National Guard and other events, not even black ministers dared take a public stand. Neither Daisy Bates nor my father persuaded many other black pastors to speak out for school integration. Where the middle-class white ministers were concerned to a large degree with maintaining and augmenting the financial resources of their churches, black ministers were constrained by fear for the well-being of their people. Thus few really stuck their necks out. If a black pastor took a public stand, people in his church would get fired by their white bosses. Most black women in the community worked as domestics in white homes. That stark reality struck all of the parents of the Little Rock Nine. Half were actually fired. Julia Ray, one of the first social workers hired by the state of Arkansas, was dismissed right off. Jeff Thomas's father was let go from his job after ten years with the International Harvester Company. A local white dentist gave him clean-up work, and that together with two other menial jobs allowed him to stay in Little Rock and remain close to his son at Central High. Melba Pattillo's mother, a high school English teacher in North Little Rock, was summoned to the principal's office and summarily given a notice of termination. It was only after Mrs. Pattillo took her story to the newspapers and to court that the principal called her back in and rehired her for the coming academic year—with no word of apology, no acknowledgment of having dismissed her a few weeks earlier.

As of September 4, unsolicited financial donations began pouring in from all parts of the United States. With them my father led in the establishment of a scholarship fund for students, both black and white he insisted, who faced "unusual stress in the school integration crisis." Later my father observed to me: "There are two types of ministers: statesmen and crusaders." With this scholarship fund—which he cited often in later years as an important achievement—he saw himself as a crusader.

A black pastor, more than a white pastor, was looked upon by his congregation as a guiding figure. Black pastors had a hold on their congregations that they did not wish to loosen. This hold included financial control. Usually better educated than most of their church members, they and their people wanted to educate their own children, and many black parents and teachers were not so sure that sending their children to a white school was a desirable move for the well-being of their children or families.

The Thursday Group

Among the parents of the Little Rock Nine, the injury of reprisal in the workplace could not compare with the anguish they began to experience at home as their children returned from school each day to tell about how—closed off behind white school doors—they were struggling to survive an incessant onslaught by some fifty of the two thousand Central High students. White students spat in their faces, tripped them, fired paperclips at their heads with rubber bands, threw metal objects wadded in paper, knocked their books out of their arms, banged them into their lockers, kicked them, and stepped on their heels and shoved them down stairs. "They throw rocks, they spill ink on your clothes," recalled Minnijean Brown, "they just keep bothering you every five minutes."[5]

Elizabeth Eckford shielded her parents by not divulging details of her abuse. In 2001 Elizabeth told me, "To her dying day, my mother never knew of the physical and verbal abuse. My father is still living. He still thinks there was some pushing and shoving. That's all." She protected her parents, but it came at a price. Her silence at home contributed to her isolation. "I could not share the daily abuse with anyone or seek justice. In school a white was afraid to sit by me or talk with me because the abuse would turn on him." That isolation, day after day, proved to be her worst trial. Once a white girl reached out to her. She and Ann Williams were in a French class together. Ann would turn around and talk to Elizabeth "like a normal person." Elizabeth still recalls Ann as her only white friend from the Central High days.

Students tormented Elizabeth in the classrooms and in the jammed halls. Between classes, like everyone else, she would go to her locker and open it to get her books. Out of the stream of passing students a couple of boys would give each other a signal and suddenly lurch over and throw their full weight against her open locker door—the height of a person—body slamming her into its narrow metal sides and jagged catches. The body slams came daily. At lunch in the cafeteria, when she walked balancing a bowl of hot soup on a tray, people would shove chairs into her legs to make her fall. At home she explained the cuts and bruises as various accidents in the street.

Daily, like hunted animals, the black students would seek refuge in a teacher's office, always wary, alert to danger, on the lookout for the minute when it was safe to move down a hallway. Only someone subjected to steady abuse as a child can know the grind of its relentlessness.

Forty years later Elizabeth observed, "Nowadays everyone says 'I didn't see anything. I didn't witness any of those incidents. I didn't know what was going on.'"

Everybody—fellow students standing next to her—did see and turned away. Central High has long, curving halls so you cannot look all the way from one end to the other. Teachers did not watch out from the hall doors of their classrooms. Rarely did a student act alone to play a mean trick. Moreover, Elizabeth feels that adults, many of them Central High parents, incited incidents. Parents furnished students with printed racist materials for in-school distribution.

The Nine also report that they ran up against racist attitudes on the part of administrators every day. One afternoon, Melba's mother saw a boy out in the school yard take a run at Melba from behind, draw his leg back as if on a soccer ball, and hurl a vicious kick into her. Melba bent double and fell. Her mother got her into the car and then rushed into the principal's office. She reported the incident. But the principal, Jess Matthews, stuck by his rule: He could and would do nothing unless the incident was witnessed by a faculty member.

Elizabeth and the other girls among the Nine had dealings chiefly with the vice principal for girls, Elizabeth Huckaby. It was their sense that whenever she received a report of harassment, she simply did not pass it along. In fact, in her memoir, *Crisis at Central High*,

"MRS" DAISY BATES

Little Rock's "Lady" of The Year

(SEE POLICE RECORD BELOW)

CENTRAL HIGH SCHOOL'S MOST PROMINENT P.T.A. MEMBER, SELF-APPOINTED PROTECTOR OF NINE NEGRO CHILDREN, HAVING RECEIVED "SUBPOENA" POWERS FROM JESS MATTHEWS, CENTRAL HIGH SCHOOL PRINCIPAL, AND ALSO AUTHORITY TO CROSS EXAMINE WHITE STUDENTS, UNOFFICIAL "PRINCIPAL" IN CHARGE OF LECTURING WHITE STUDENTS AT CENTRAL HIGH WHO "CROSS" ANY OF HER "BRAVE" NINE NEGRO STUDENTS.

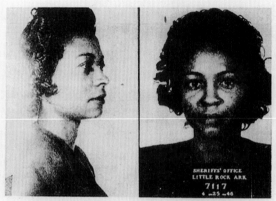

DAISY BATES - SHERIFF'S OFFICE PHOTOS

Form SP-104—10M—1-57—136018

DEPARTMENT OF ARKANSAS STATE POLICE
HERMAN E. LINDSEY, Director
Little Rock, Arkansas

IDENTIFICATION & RECORDS
CAPT. LEON GERSHNER

The following is a transcript of the record, including the most recently reported data, as shown in the files of this Bureau concerning our number: 130846

1914 Ark. DF   BATES, Daisy Lee 10- I R III 3
FBI#4590725   I U III 3

Contributor of Fingerprints	Name and Number	Arrested or Received	Charge	Disposition
PD Monroe, La.	Daisey Bates #1885	11-16-34	Inv.	rel
SO Little Rock,Ark.	Daisy Lee Bates #7117	4-25-46	contempt of court	
PD,Little Rock,Ark.	Daisey Lee Bates #10663	4-25-46	contempt	.100. and 10 das record received from SO Little Rock,Ark.
PD,Little Rock,Ark.	Daisy Bates case #449	1-26-52	Gaming	5.00 & cost
PD,Little Rock,Ark	Daisy Bates Case 446	11-2-57	Failure to Regy. NAACP	Pending to 12-3-57

PARENTS: DO YOU KNOW . . . .

1. THERE IS A VICIOUS FEAR CAMPAIGN IN PROCESS AT CENTRAL HIGH SCHOOL, WHEREBY THE WHITE CHILDREN ARE BEING TOLD THAT AT ANYTIME A WHITE CHILD HAS TROUBLE WITH A NEGRO STUDENT THAT THE WHITE STUDENTS MUST FACE DAISY BATES AND BE CROSS-EXAMINED BY HER.
2. THAT AN IRON-CLAD CENSORSHIP HAS BEEN CLAMPED ON CENTRAL HIGH SCHOOL.
3. JESS MATTHEWS, PRINCIPAL, HAS IMPOSED AN ALMOST PRISON-LIKE FEAR UPON THE WHITE STUDENTS AGAINST TALKING EVEN TO THEIR PARENTS ABOUT WHAT IS GOING ON IN CENTRAL HIGH SCHOOL.
4. THAT DAISY BATES HAS FREE ACCESS TO THE SCHOOL AND JESS MATTHEWS' OFFICE, AND IS SEEN FREQUENTLY IN MATTHEWS' OFFICE.
5. THAT DAISY BATES WAS ALLOWED TO CROSS-EXAMINE A NUMBER OF WHITE STUDENTS RECENTLY FOLLOWING A KICK-FIGHT BETWEEN A WHITE GIRL AND A NEGRO GIRL. BECAUSE THE WHITE GIRL WOULD NOT ANSWER DAISY BATES' QUESTIONS, MR. MATTHEWS GAVE THE WHITE GIRL TWO WEEKS IN THE DETENTION HALL.

WHO IS RUNNING CENTRAL HIGH SCHOOL?
BLOSSOM OR BATES? .. OR BOTH!

Paid for and distributed by Capital Citizens Council, Julian Miller, Director

Vice Principal Huckaby even goes so far as to criticize several of the Nine—for being too tentative (Jeff) or too impulsive (Minnijean) or too aggressive (Melba).[6]

I asked Elizabeth, "Why did you stick it out?"

She told me, "At first education stood as a high family ideal. Teachers were gods to my parents, especially my mother. Then half-way through the 1957–1958 year, things got really awful and Minnijean was expelled, and I thought, 'I am doing something for my race.' My parents talked that way. Also my grandparents."

I objected, "That's still too intellectual. Deep down inside you, what kept you in that school?"

Elizabeth said, "I'm a shy person. I follow authority. But sometimes I dig in my heels. I didn't want to let down the other Nine. Once I called home and said, 'I've had enough. Come and get me.' My father came and got me. But next day I went back. I did not want to let the others down."

Daisy Bates had the Nine meet at her home every day after school until about halfway through the year. From the beginning she instructed them over and over, "Do not talk [outside] about the mistreatment." Only in the confines of her house and only in each others' company were they to vent their hurt and rage. Carlotta Walls admitted that the Nine would joke about these things among themselves in order to keep their spirits up and that they would withhold from their parents much of what was really going on. Minnijean said that each time Orval Faubus or Amis Guthridge—attorney for the White Citizens Council and the Central High Mothers League[7]—made a speech: "We knew we were going to get it. The incidents would get worse. We'd kid about it, and say we'd go and buy knee pads because we knew we were going to get kicked, pushed, cursed, and have hot soup spilled on us by white students."

Under these circumstances academic achievement would seem a miracle. Yet by year's end Gloria Ray's prize-winning science project would be featured in local papers and Carlotta Walls would make the honor roll. At the after-school sessions Ernest Green, the senior among them, played the buoyant big brother. He would make light of his abuse or crack a joke about his tormentors.

(Opposite): Arkansas State Police file on Daisy Bates—adapted as flyer distributed by white students at Central High, Fall 1957.

Not until 1994, three and a half decades later, could Melba Pattillo (Beals) bring herself to publish her diary from those days, *Warriors Don't Cry*, and talk about her inside-the-school experiences, and only after forty years could Elizabeth Eckford start to talk about it.

Leaders of the NAACP in Little Rock asked my father to organize an interracial group to support in particular the parents of the Nine and to create a gathering place for others at the forefront of the conflict. They would come to call it simply the Thursday Group. They chose my father for reasons they knew well. From the day he had arrived in Little Rock, he had begun visiting in the homes of the black community at all socioeconomic levels. His rounds through hospital wards included regular weekly appearances at the bedsides of black patients in the Negro Ward of the Arkansas Baptist Hospital. He would present them with sections of Sunday papers and magazines. His church had sponsored a black Presbyterian church in town. Eventually, he was the man who persuaded the family of Terrence Roberts, one of the Nine, to allow a Canadian filmmaker into their home in order to shoot a civil rights film.

Daisy Bates always came to the Thursday Group. The parents brought their personal agonies. A meeting would start at 10:00 a.m. and last a couple of hours. My father described the immediacy: "Interested white and Negro citizens worked to protest harassment of Negro students inside of Central High School. Out of this developed a discussion and prayer group which met weekly throughout the extended crisis to discuss and act helpfully on the situation in the community. Here in this group the concepts of inferiority, superiority, condescension, and reserve all disappeared. For here were people, all under like attack, and all united in a common struggle." [8] They never missed a week, except Christmas. Attendance ranged from fifteen to forty.

My father and Daisy Bates must get credit as pioneers in this kind of regular gathering for mutual support. The group met every Thursday morning at the Dunbar Community Center (named for black poet Paul Laurence Dunbar, as were many black institutions in the South), already a focal point for the black populace, where as my father said they "worked in a quiet way for civil rights." Discussion helped to clarify their thinking and give each other courage. It served as a launching place for the black parents' participation in the Parent-Teacher Association at Central High. Sometimes they called it

A Thursday Group meeting, Little Rock, spring 1958. Ogden at end of table with his back to camera and Daisy Bates at far end of table. (Printed in *Jet*, June 12, 1958.)

the Thursday Morning Prayer Meeting. They would begin by joining hands around a table and saying the Lord's Prayer or inviting each who wished to offer a brief prayer. If future generations emulate to their profit any single element from this crisis, it will be the Thursday Group.

My mother always attended. She said, "The parents of the children felt they could come and they wouldn't be harassed by the police or anybody. They were afraid at night. A few of them told us they kept guns under their pillows, afraid some white people would attack them. But this was a place where they could express their fears to some white people. Those parents, you felt so—you felt sort of help-less. What can I say to these parents whose child is in this dangerous situation day after day after day? They talked about practical things like how to answer hate calls." She remembered, "One day, you see, all the children went to Daisy Bates's home after school and they'd tell about what had happened to them and so on. One day Dad and I went too. Daisy Bates took me down into the basement where these nine children—maybe eight—were sitting around, and she said, 'Talk to them.'

"I said to them, 'I can understand to some extent what you young people are going through. But don't let hate take over in your lives, because that is the most damaging thing that can happen to you. These people are exhibiting a lot of hate, but don't let this grow in you.'"

Eleanor Roosevelt, in a *Boston Daily Globe* article about Little Rock, assessed the situation of the black parents quite accurately.[9] "The fathers and mothers must have felt most fearful when they took their children to enter those hostile schools. I sometimes wonder how many of us ever consider how it would feel if we found ourselves among a hostile mob of people of other races and colors." Four years later, as the civil rights movement continued, a support group like the Thursday morning gathering in Little Rock would become standard procedure, but the pioneers in 1957 were inventing and improvising as they went along.

My father told a reporter later: "People said there was no communication any more between whites and Negroes in Little Rock. It just wasn't so. There was—each week in that group. A real communication such as there had never been before. We became true friends. The racial barriers all fell away." Later on it came to be called Meeting for Conversation. It continued at the Dunbar Community Center, wrote Nat Griswold, until 1960—"for two hours each Thursday morning uninhibited interaction among concerned Negroes and whites."[10]

My father had long felt that "it was probably inevitable that something similar to the Little Rock crisis would happen somewhere in the South. There were wrong attitudes between two groups of people in the South. It was as if these attitudes were moisture in suspension in the air. The climate changed in Little Rock, precipitation followed, and the chill rain fell. Conversely, there were—in the hearts and minds of some others who became part of the weekly prayer and discussion group—right attitudes of love and appreciation of one's fellow human beings. When the climate changed, these two crystallized."

In addition, during the tense opening days of September, my father issued an official appeal to all members of the Ministerial As-

Thurgood Marshall, NAACP chief counsel, holds the door for Daisy Bates, with Gloria Ray and Minnijean Brown as they exit from the Little Rock Federal District courtroom. (Photograph by Will Counts.)

sociation urging their congregations to comply peacefully with the federal court orders. When Faubus surrounded Central High with the National Guard, my father initiated a public denouncement of the action, and sixteen local ministers joined in the denouncement. Immediately after Integration Wednesday, September 4, 1957, he set about, as he wrote, "calling for ministers of all denominations and races to come together at the Y.W.C.A. in Little Rock . . . at a time when such a meeting might have been the object of fierce hostility." The YWCA, along with the Dunbar Community Center, served as a major social gathering place for black citizenry. "We have to go ahead under opposition," he told them. The resulting statewide meeting of clergymen, which he organized and moderated—some fifty pastors, from fourteen communities and nine denominations—released a pro-integration statement to the press. "We have too readily treated the present situation as though it were a Constitutional crisis alone, and not also a religious and moral crisis."

He knew an even more violent day was about to erupt over at Central High. How to care for his congregation and bring them with him? On Sunday, September 22, he began defining his sermon topic with his characteristic elaborateness: "From time to time," he said to

School integration protesters march toward Central High. (Photograph by Will Counts; his "favorite" 1957–1958 Little Rock photo.)

his people, "we come to some special experience of difficulty, some hour of testing, some place of choosing, some cross roads of decision which we may call *a crisis*."

That Sunday's church bulletin announced an ongoing ironic counterpoint at Central Presbyterian to the integration furor: "Miss Emily Boehler will show slides and tell of her work as a missionary in Africa." Central Presbyterian was her home church. Emily Boehler was their very own missionary whom they supported to educate black children on another continent.

The Bateses' *State Press* printed two photographs of the events at Central High the next morning, September 23, on its front page. One was of a white man leaping onto the back of a black man wearing a suit and grabbing him around the neck in a choke hold. The picture

Mob attacks Alex Wilson, black journalist, in front of Central High, September 23, 1957. (Photograph by Will Counts.)

beneath showed another white man from the same mob delivering a kick to the kidneys of the same black man. The place was Central High. The black man was L. Alex Wilson, managing editor of the *Tri-state Defender,* the black newspaper of Memphis. He had come with three other black journalists to cover the story of a renewed attempt by the Little Rock Nine to enter Central High. Wilson wrote afterward, "I was abused—the victim of misguided violence, but I am not bitter." Three years later he would die of the injuries.

About a thousand people had gathered that Monday morning. My father went over and mingled with the crowd, as he often would during the subsequent months. NAACP field secretary Frank Smith and the lawyer C. C. Mercer (with Daisy Bates in his car) each drove a carload of the Nine to a side entrance of the school. With enormous courage the four black newspapermen arriving at the front of the school turned themselves into decoys and made the clandestine side-door entry possible for the children. Someone spotted the children as they entered: "They're in! The niggers are in!"

During those same hours my father went to Mayor Wilson Mann and to Chief of Police Marvin Potts with a written appeal to take control of the rioting mob, an appeal he had led the Ministerial Association to issue. Of the interracial fifty-one clergy he could gather, thirty-eight had signed. He managed to present it in person. It was their "urgent request that the law enforcement powers of the city, county, and state disperse the crowds of people in front of Central High." He called the day "Black Monday."

Throughout his ministry in Little Rock, my father enjoyed courteous, working contacts with the all-white police force, ranging from cooperation at civic functions to help with needy people whom they had picked up. He was a man they would phone. In turn, he at times would intercede on behalf of a detainee. He was always calling around, seeking a job for someone newly released from prison.

In late June 1958, my father would lead a delegation of five citizens and two police sergeants from Little Rock to the 1958 Institute on Police and Community Relations at Texas A&M College. During the 1957–1958 turmoil he worked steadily, in asking police protection for Daisy and L. C. Bates and others, requesting fair treatment and fair play—all while walking a personal tightrope, knowing full well that he and his own family lived under police surveillance. In public he and Police Chief Potts held each other in respect. But in private my father regarded Chief Potts as "a hard-boiled man": As a friend confided, "He'd call him a racist cop if he weren't a preacher." Potts resigned in October 1957 and a remarkable man named Gene Smith replaced him.

Officer Smith, with a hundred of his best men, had held back the surging mob of a thousand at Central High on the morning of September 23, Smith like "a one-man army," wrote the *New York Times*. But around 11:00 a.m. the barricades broke, and by 11:30 a.m. the city police could no longer control the mob. Smith and school officials hustled the Nine out of Central High through a delivery entrance in the rear of the school and drove them in police cars to their homes.[11]

The ministers' appeal may have given the mayor the final courage to call for the help of federal troops. The next day, on September 24,

101st Airborne paratroopers accompany the Nine to Central High, September 25, 1957. (Photograph by Will Counts.)

President Eisenhower issued an executive order placing the National Guard under federal command. Then he ordered a thousand paratroopers from the 101st Airborne Division of the U.S. Army to leave Fort Campbell, Kentucky, and go to Little Rock. That night jeeps, half-tracks, and convoy trucks began grinding their way through the streets of Little Rock. Around Central High they stacked their rifles and pitched their tents. On the morning of September 25, the U.S. Army took the Nine to school and, according to the *State Press*, "calmness" marked the day.

My father "publicly praised the move," wrote a pair of sociologists who had come to town to study the situation. "He was virtually the only local leader to do so."[12] On that day and on every day, as long as federal troops surrounded Central High, the black students were driven in army vehicles the twenty blocks between the Bateses' home and Central High. Sometimes the morning pickup occurred at a parents' home, varying the routine in order to avoid attack. The Nine entered and exited the school amid a phalanx of soldiers. Inside the building each of the Nine was assigned an individual soldier as bodyguard, allowed in the hallways but not in the classrooms or bathrooms.[13]

On Sunday, September 29, my father spoke from his pulpit with a force highly uncharacteristic of a man who prided himself on his public control. The next day's *Arkansas Gazette* carried the story, "Those Who Favor Christian Principles and Law Should Speak Up, Little Rock Minister Declares." He had decided to forgo oblique references in favor of direct discourse.

His message on that Sunday predicted a new voice and new style born of new thinking that evolved as a result of the brutality. His sermon, "The Teachings of Christ for Our Times," stressed the *teachings* of Jesus. By the end of the school year his sermons would stress the *actions* of Jesus. He started this sermon on September 29 with a passage from Amos: "Justice shall roll down like waters, and righteousness as a mighty stream." He called the line a plea for fair treatment. By the end of the school year, he would declaim the same passage again, calling it a command from the mouth of God.

On September 29, he knew that members of his congregation would walk out. They had already begun to split apart, hard. Still, he told them straight out: "Sometimes a church goes through a screening process. God shows which are truly *Christian in a certain area of life*" (my father's underlining in his sermon notes). The present period he saw as "such a testing time." He continued with an attack on the small-minded bickering he heard around him: "Some people are so concerned with church plans, or adorning the church sanctuary, or arranging the church furniture. . . ." From his pulpit he went on as quoted by the *Gazette*: "We who approve of the present beginning of gradual integration in the Little Rock High Schools, either as a matter of high Christian principles, or because it is now the law of the land, should find ways to give expression to our views." He exhorted his congregation: Telephone, write, pray. He named names, including "the extreme segregationist Mothers League of Central High School." He took to task the people who wanted to stop the mouths of their preachers, again summoning the prophet Amos's fierce denunciation of people in his own day: "Ye commanded the prophets, saying, prophesy not." My father finished his sermon that morning with

Jesus's final command to his disciples to go out and teach. He then stepped down to the floor of the church sanctuary and conducted the annual fall dedication ceremony for all teachers about to lead Sunday School classes during the year, from nursery and kindergarten through high school and senior adults.

The Friendly Church and the Neighborhood

Founded in 1894, Central Presbyterian Church on Arch Street was a neighborhood church. Its fiftieth-anniversary pamphlet celebrated it as "The Friendly Church." But by 1957 the neighborhood was suddenly and rapidly changing. With the recent slum clearing by the federally funded Little Rock Housing Authority and the new urban renewal, blacks had begun to cross over Roosevelt Avenue and move into streets where only whites had lived. Fifteen blocks from Central Presbyterian, Central High with its football stadium stood on grounds soon to be surrounded by black families only. The once clean, well-cut lawns and fresh single-family houses were beginning to show weeds, peeling paint, and tatty curtains. Here and there the iron balustrades were rusting and the roofs leaking on the extravagant Victorian wood and brick structures. Now Central Presbyterian was positioned on the front line of the area that divided black and white Little Rock, the homes of my father's parishioners, together with the manse (the church-owned house where the pastor lives) at 1863 Chester Street, located right in the transition zone.

The white family next door prepared to sell their house to a black family. Before the information went public, a real estate agent who had gotten wind of the impending sale called my father and suggested that he convince his church to dispose of 1863 Chester quickly or its value would drop drastically. "Eventually the other houses on the block will bring much less?" asked my father.

"That's exactly it," she said.

"Do you call this Christian?"

"I don't know whether it's Christian or not but that's the way it's done."

"No," said my father, "I have to refuse your plan." For one thing, the sale would have weakened his pro-integration position. Together with elders Marion Crist and Gardner Lile, he was able to persuade the church to keep the manse.

Central Presbyterian Church, on Arch Street,
Little Rock, Ogden's pastorate, 1954–1958.

A black couple bought the house next door. "One hot night after the sale," remembered my mother, "the windows were open
between our houses and we could hear them talking in their bedroom. She was saying to her husband, 'Aren't you glad we have *quiet*
neighbors.'"[14]

Most of the five hundred members of Central Presbyterian Church
lived nearby, although with the increasing number of automobiles in
the early 1950s people were beginning to move out of the neighborhood or attend a church at some distance if, for instance, members
of their family lived in another part of town. The members of Central Presbyterian were middle-class people of modest means. Many
of the men earned their living selling real estate, investments, or insurance; some worked in construction and engineering; several were

members of labor unions. One member of the Session (the church's organization of elected elders) was an office manager for the Lion Oil Company, another a salesman at Montgomery Ward, another a paperhanger and house painter. A handful of women in the church were active or retired teachers. In those days women were not elected to the Session or the Board of Deacons. No church member sat on the Little Rock School Board. Gardner Lile was a banker; his friend Marion T. Crist a city engineer. The position and income of each of these two men made him an anomaly in the socioeconomic profile of my father's church. Crist served on the board of Stillman College, a black college in Tuscaloosa, Alabama. Crist would eventually fly my father in his private plane to the San Francisco Bay Area to give talks about the racial issue. It was out of loyalty that Crist and Lile and their families, with earlier roots in the neighborhood, chose to stay on.

The forces of integration affected businessmen in real estate and insurance most dramatically, and threatened blue-collar workers. Local labor union leaders opposed black entry into unions. These were the men of my father's church. My father's parishioners were not merchants, bankers, or other professionals who felt little or no impact from the new agitation in the black community.

When my father first walked with the Nine and then continued, as it were, to do so, he placed his congregation in an excruciating dilemma. On the one hand, he stood for what he thought was right, he taught his people from the Bible, and by his very position as their pastor he carried a special weight of authority about him. On the other hand, by his recent actions and teaching, and now through his use of his position as their pastor, he seemed to be destroying their livelihood and their neighborhood.

Years later a member of Central Presbyterian from those days put it to me like this. "No church members wanted their pastor to go meddling in other people's affairs. That's not his business. He is their pastor, in their church. From their pulpit his job is to conduct services, to preach love and brotherhood, and do things according to procedure. In fact, if he followed the rules in all other matters, he could have a fairly free pulpit to say whatever he wished." One of the major financial contributors to my father's church said, "This integration business is not exactly what his congregation pays him for." In the people of his flock he triggered the threat of losing their church, the dread of losing their homes, the anxiety of losing their jobs, and, eventually through interracial dating, the fear of losing their children. Normally, clergymen and schoolmen followed businessmen, rather than leading them, but now a major socioeconomic upheaval had reversed that order.

Meanwhile in the fall of 1957 hundreds of reporters and photojournalists were arriving in town, black as well as white. Dark-skinned journalists poured into Little Rock from their New York and New England papers, from the Deep South, from British news services, from the African press with Egypt and Rhodesia (Zambia, Zimbabwe) and from Pakistan and India and Ceylon (Sri Lanka). They had nowhere to gather. All hotels and motels remained off-limits to them because they were "black." Only the airport restaurant would serve blacks. The offices of the *Arkansas Gazette* and *Democrat* never opened their doors to them, nor did the Little Rock Press Club across the street. Newspeople of different racial groups never visited at each others' desks in the publishing building, or smoked together, or borrowed each others' typewriters. Even forty years later at the anniversary celebration of the integration of Central High, no African American journalist would be invited to the stage of Central High's auditorium to speak at the journalists' public reunion. In the fall and winter of 1957, many of the dark-skinned reporters from out of town slept at Daisy and L. C. Bates's house and typed out their stories there. And at many a midnight they crowded into my parents' little living room, chairs jammed along the walls, my mother's coffee cups in hand. She said she "made gallons of coffee and hot chocolate, and sandwiches."

White reporters sat there as well, listening to my father, who had become a major source of information and perspective. "It was one of the few friendly places they could go," said my father, "because most people took the attitude that the newspaper men were not going to give to the world a report of the Little Rock school situation that would show the segregationists in a very good light." In interviews with journalists, from the beginning my father always stressed the fairness issue. Repeatedly he insisted, "Central High offers about fifty courses not offered at Horace Mann, the Negro high school, that satisfy prerequisites for admission to the better colleges and universities in the Northeast." He was a man who dwelled on hard evidence and fact.

On Sunday, October 6, the *Gazette* ran a feature story on him. "It was not to be expected that all who are associated with me would agree with all my views," he told the journalist, Roy Reed. "However, the members of our congregation have given evidence of being united in love and loyalty to our church and of desiring to do the most Christian and brotherly thing in the matter of race relations." His cautious verb—"have given evidence"—hints at the tension. He was fighting to keep his people in his church while battling the racism outside its walls.

On October 12, 1957, Protestant, Catholic, and Jewish clergymen sponsored a citywide interfaith Day of Prayer. An estimated eighty-four separate meetings were held. More than eight thousand people attended. Over at Central High, one thousand federal troops and eighty-five hundred rotating, federalized National Guardsmen kept the peace. The clergymen planning the event suggested that the prayers include pleas for

- forgiveness for having left undone things that ought to have been done
- the support and preservation of law and order
- the leaders of the community, the state, and nation
- the youth in the schools and community
- the casting out of rancor and prejudice in favor of understanding and compassion
- resistance against unthinking agitators

In no way did these goals separate segregationists from integrationists. Both groups could pray ardently for all of the items as a means to their diametrically opposed goals. The chief sponsor, Episcopalian Bishop Robert R. Brown, proclaimed the prayer list as commencing a "Ministry of Reconciliation," of forgiveness not judgment. President Eisenhower and Governor Orval Faubus publicly endorsed it, the latter writing that "Your attitude of seeking to bring about reconciliation rather than attempting to place blame is the proper approach at this time." Bishop Brown was pleased, he told *Time* magazine, with the open witness by Arkansans to "their belief in law and order."

But according to a pair of sociologists from the Harvard Laboratory of Social Relations, with that Day of Prayer the possibility for the clergy of Little Rock to lead a genuine movement toward racial justice ended. Ernest Campbell and Thomas Pettigrew had come to town to do research for a book on the Little Rock clergy in crisis.

In effect, eyewitnesses Campbell and Pettigrew wrote in 1958, as of October 12, 1957, clergy and congregations exerted no influence on the course of integration. With rare exceptions, impact on integration could be brought to bear only through nonchurch organizations. "After these prayers, most of the ministerial participants ceased their integrationist activity completely. But Action [their code name for my father] continued unabated." And, the researchers noted, "many of his closest ministerial friends let him go it alone."[15]

Not only did the Brown Day of Prayer prove ineffective in the cause of peace, but much more seriously it siphoned off what potential there was for effective church action. Talking with me later, my father reflected, "From every pulpit ministers pray for peace and preach brotherhood. They proclaim the example of Jesus. Most Presbyterians even stand up and say publicly they are for racial justice. But then they say, 'We must be careful in this matter of school integration. We must proceed with caution.' They *never, never* come right out and say, 'I *approve* of those nine Negro children entering Central High School today. It is the right thing to do.' " The citizens of Little Rock, especially parents of white high school students, were dividing into two distinct, vocal factions, and their churches naturally reflected that split.

Out in town pro-Faubus parents shouted,

Two, four, six, eight,
We ain't gonna integrate.

Pro-integrationists chanted back,

Eight, six, four, two,
Ten to one, I bet you do.

Two days after the Guard had turned back the Nine, Daisy and L. C. Bates's newspaper—the *State Press*—reprimanded its black readers, as it would throughout the year: "It is unfortunate that Negroes put Faubus in office." Financial incentives and threats of job loss had been brought to bear on the black populace. The burden of the paper's demand to its subscribers: pay the poll tax and vote. Every issue of the *State Press* attempted to rally blacks not only in Little Rock but in neighboring, predominantly black communities, some with names such as Dew Drop, Dollarway, Smackover, Sunshine, and Sweet Home.

The Ku Klux Klan staged three separate cross-burning episodes on the Bateses' lawn during the year. They reminded the black community that the last Little Rock lynching, near the center of town, had occurred only thirty years earlier. Members of the black community remembered. White opposition also came from the local branch of the White Citizens Council, from gatherings of conservative white clergy, and from a group that called itself the Mothers League of Central High School. They took their cause to the courts and to the school board. (Only one member of the school board would stay on after the year was over.) These groups organized protest actions, and they set up telephone networks. "You better get those coons out of that school," Daisy Bates would hear as she lifted her phone receiver.

They bombarded my parents' home with hate calls and hate mail. My father soon confessed that when taking on the presidency of the Ministerial Association, he had no inkling of the trouble he was in for. From then on, when anyone opposed the integrationist position or suspected integrationist position of any church, they called or wrote to my father. He was the public figure. He was on the spot.

They went after him at home and at church. The regular church secretary could not take it any more and quit. So my mother had to step in—fielding calls, connecting people for church functions, organizing and mimeographing the bulletin for each Sunday with its order of service and announcements. She went on doing that from September through the following July. All of a sudden, former friends avoided my mother. Church people with whom she had sung in the choir and with whom she had worked in the women's church circles would cross the street rather than speak to her.

Anyone who would snub my mother has to have been possessed by demonic rage or fear. Throughout the sixty years that I knew her, people warmed to her—more so than to my father—and their affection for her lasted. My father would feel that, and, in admiration of my mother, he would comment on it to us boys. "Your mother," he would say. "People just love your mother. People are

naturally attracted to her. I think people like her better than me."
Later in Berkeley a young immigrant Japanese woman in my parents'
church adopted her as her mother and called her "Mother" to the end
of her days.

It was my mother who held the family together. She possessed a
keen intellect that emerged always with simple modesty, a genuine
shyness, an enduring common sense, and an inner strength nour-
ished by deep religious faith. She was not given to the kind of ques-
tionings that punctuated my father's religious life, and her natural,
self-effacing attitude put her husband in the spotlight to such a degree that when she and my father were together at public or social
events, many people did not remember her presence. When clinical
depression struck my father again, in 1951, and this time he had to
resign from his church in Staunton, Virginia, it was my mother who
consulted with doctors in the community and on their advice put
him in Johns Hopkins. It was she who then single-handedly packed
up the household, closed the manse, and moved to her own mother's
in Springfield, Ohio, with two-year-old Paul.

In our home, twice each year, as far back as I can remember,
the same scene played out in front of our kitchen wall calendar. It
started with Jonathan. It continued with Paul. It would happen in
Little Rock: my mother standing between Paul and my father, each
demanding her attention and everyone pointing to the calendar and
talking passionately. As the summer vacation and the Christmas vacation period would come to an end, Paul would begin protesting
against having to leave home and return to his school in St. Louis.
Like his brother Jonathan before him, Paul's objections would grow
each day in vehemence and tearfulness. A little ritual would follow.
My mother would take Jonathan, and now Paul, over to the calendar
and turn the sheets, showing him that "in a few weeks"—she would
count them with him—he would come back home. At the same time,
in the Little Rock house something of the utmost urgency would
have just come up for my father. He would be pointing to the coming week on the kitchen calendar and asking her advice about "how
to handle"—say—an impending crisis discussion he and Daisy Bates
needed to initiate at their next support group meeting with the parents of the Nine, the "Thursday Group." He would have just received
"an emergency telephone call" and would have to make some phone

calls "right away." In the household, my mother stood between Paul's demands and my father's like a suspension bridge.

My father's stamina firmed itself on my mother's balance and took hold in her judgment. He relied on the bedrock that she was. Her faith, sense of humor, respect for other people, and pragmatism got my father through not only the episodes of depression and the deafness of two sons, but his church crisis as well.

At the Little Rock church she also sang in the choir and sometimes substituted as church organist. It was her independence of spirit and ability to take action that had won her entrance to the Cincinnati Conservatory of Music. She had graduated there in piano—and at graduation won the Bach Prize for composition—back in the days when Cincinnati and Juilliard were the two powerhouses for musical training in the United States. As a senior she had been selected to play the Mendelssohn Piano Concerto with the Conservatory Orchestra.

One of the ironies life delivered to this gifted musician was her pair of deaf sons, my younger brothers Jonathan and Paul, both totally deaf at birth due to retinitis pigmentosa—the product of a freak mix of my parents' recessive genes that their generation knew nothing about. When Jonathan and, then, much later, Paul were toddlers, she would not sit at the piano and play while they were awake because they would see her doing something they could not grasp. I did not know that until she told me many years later. She never made a point of it with any of the rest of the family.

Sometimes, in a dark philosophical mood, my father would ask, "Why did God give us deaf sons? Why? Why? Why?" and my mother would always ask, always in a practical mood, "What are we going to do about it?" It is testimony to my parents' partnership and searching nature that they took baby Jonathan to the finest clinics they could find to test his deafness and then, though the Virginia State School for the Deaf stood right in our town of Staunton, they sent off Jonathan at age six to Central Institute for the Deaf, a thousand miles away in St. Louis, because their research told them that it was one of only two schools in the nation that taught exclusively lipreading and speaking. They felt that without lipreading and speaking, a deaf person would be isolated from the hearing world.

It is testimony to my mother's pragmatic nature that once they discovered that Jonathan was deaf, she set about gathering all the information she could in order to teach him. She would take three-by-five cards and print the names of objects in the house on them and tape them on the "table," "chair," "refrigerator," "mailbox"—everywhere. Later she said that in those early years she felt she did not know enough to start the deaf boys in voice and speech, but clearly she started them with lipreading. She told me several times about her great victory moment with Paul. She said that he loved taking a bath upstairs in the bathtub. One afternoon, while she was sitting in the living room where he was playing, she turned to him and enunciated, "Do you want to take a bath?" Paul must have been four or five. "His little face just broke out in smiles," she told me. "He jumped up and raced up the stairs and started turning on the water in the bathtub. He had understood what I had said!" That would be one of my rare glimpses of tears welling up in my mother's eyes.

At every meal she would turn her head to Jonathan, and later to Paul, and mouth every word every person said. She would also do that whenever guests visited in our home. We would sit in the living room and as we talked, she would always turn her head and repeat for Jonathan, and later for Paul, each word that was being spoken, no matter how unimportant. She would do that when the TV was on and even when we went to the movies. When eventually my brother Paul finished at Central Institute for the Deaf in St. Louis and came home to attend a hearing high school, my mother got the textbooks and tutored him in subjects such as math and Latin.

Striving for objectivity as I look at youthful pictures of her, I still think that they show a pretty young woman, slender, with dark hair, unblemished skin, a gentle nose, lively dark eyes, and fine subtle lips that would be easy for a deaf person to read. My father used to say to us, "Your mother has the loveliest shoulders," as he would walk over to where she was standing and pass his hand over her shoulder blades.

She said to us often that she had married him "because he was so affectionate, and I missed that from both my parents." And, as far as we boys could see, he was. When we went out in winter, my father never failed to help her into her coat. And then, at the car, he would always rush around, sometimes all the way around the back of the car to the passenger side, to hold the door open for her.

She laughed a lot. She made funny little remarks, such as saying about our dog when eating, "He's gone into the kitchen to refer to his bowl." Where my father, a man of wit, invented limericks and relished puns and other wordplays, my mother's family conversation always floated on her sense of humor. Her favorite kind of joke we'd call "a shaggy dog story." She would tell one and laugh a tinkling, twinkling, contagious, face-wreathed-in-smiles laugh.

When we were children, her thrift made family trips possible in our summer vacations. On four different occasions, we all climbed in the car and drove around the United States during my father's one-month summer vacation. My parents thought that was essential for our education. She'd make up the budget and with the aid of Conoco travel guides she'd lay out the route. We boys were famous among our cousins for having driven "out West" for an entire month and never having eaten a single meal in a restaurant, never having indulged in the extravagance of even an ice cream cone. My parents would take one motel room, where she'd prepare sandwiches and oatmeal, and, with the motel owner's permission—the begging of which by my father would make me cringe ("We are traveling on a limited budget. . . .")—my brother David and I would sleep outside in the carport on cots we carried along in the trunk of the car.

In Little Rock my mother would sort through the mail and pull out and destroy the hate mail before my father could see it, "because it hurt him so," she would say.

Years later I asked her, "Did you have any fear as far as Dad was concerned? Did you think that maybe he wouldn't be able to hold up under some of the pressures that were being put on him?"

She answered, "I hoped that he would not go back into a depression. But for some reason or other—I tell you, maybe you'd say I had faith to believe that everything was going to come out all right. When he was in the midst of his depression, people would commiserate with me, and I guess the idea was, 'Maybe he'll never be able to function again, adequately.' But I didn't ever have that feeling."

My mother thought back to the onset of the depression when my father had to give up his church in Staunton, Virginia, and spend seven months in Johns Hopkins. She said, "When I went back to Staunton, there was a woman in our church who had had a depression—I didn't know this—but she came to me and she said, 'It's going to take four or five years before your husband gets over this—

because I had one and I know how long it takes.' Well, my feeling was, 'This is going to take a long time, but he is going to come out of it—because God is not going to put somebody on the shelf who has all the ability and the good that he can do from now to the end of his life, because he's not an old man, and God needs him and will use him, and so I'm sure he's going to come out all right.' I think—to me—this is part of God's working. I think that God put it into the heart of that woman to tell me her experience so that I would know what his situation was."

In that statement I find a quintessential example of links between my mother's faith and her pragmatism. With that armor she got my father through, his only daily support. Daisy Bates had L. C. Bates to get her through. My father and Daisy Bates gave each other courage.

The Bateses and the Ogdens

Letters to the editors of the local newspapers in Little Rock singled out my father as their favorite target for abuse in the white community, just as Daisy Bates became the favorite target for abuse in the black community. My father published articles and interviews in the *Gazette* and the *Democrat*. He also became quite visible when he created and then took on the chairmanship of the Goodwill Scholarship Fund "to reward youth of Little Rock Central High showing a belief in fair play"—a trust he set up with the unsolicited donations that were pouring in from all over the country. Yet another public act that brought down on him even more anger from the segregationist white community.

The phone at home never stopped ringing, with calls ranging from objections on biblical grounds to "race-mixing" and "mongrelization"—the term for segregationists' biggest terror—to out-and-out "nigger lover" name-calling. "Why is it," my father once mused to me, "that people say 'half-breed' scornfully? I've heard people say a good many times in the South that the blacker a black man is, the more likely he is to be honest. The blacker he is, the more likely you can trust him."

"Who is this?" my father would say to the anonymous caller. "You know who I am, but you refuse to tell me who you are. You're a coward. You're chicken!" he'd say. "One night," said my mother, "they called up every fifteen minutes. They must have had a whole group of people there. This went on till after midnight. Finally I put a pillow under the telephone and two or three pillows on top of it. There was no way to turn the phone off."

My parents struggled to hold themselves in check against even a hint of retaliation. At times it demanded huge self-control. "But," my father said, "I would never let myself write a letter or communicate in a call my resentment, strong as it could be, toward those people who really elicited it."

Even a few of my father's own church members phoned up to harangue him, especially a Mr. I. E. Jones, who never actually attended services but who was obsessed with the incursion of blacks into white life and who railed at my father about once a week. My father said that after taking the call he would lay aside the receiver and read the morning paper for a while and then pick it up to find Mr. Jones still going.

Eventually Mr. I. E. Jones died of lung cancer. Ever after, my mother always stressed the poetic justice in that cancer, as she did toward other freak accidents that damaged or killed harassers around the church. Later on, another member of my father's church, the "hammer of the opposition" as my mother called him, fell off a roof and broke his back, while a third, also an ardent segregationist in the church, was bitten by a black widow spider. Throughout his life my father always objected strenuously but with good humor to this element in his wife's theology. But it was mostly my mother who fielded the calls, sorted through the letters when the post was delivered, and destroyed most of the hate mail before he could see it. "It could hurt him so deeply," she said to me later. "After a while it could really get to him."

The abuse toward my father from his revered and beloved Old South could inflict the severest injury. The visiting sociologists Campbell and Pettigrew sensed his pain, noting that he talked to them "feelingly of his homeland. He speaks feelingly of how his efforts in the cause of racial justice disassociate him from a tradition and a people he loves." They go on to observe, "He does not fully understand the vigor of their caustic remarks, and their remarks are the more caustic because he was one of their own." In later life he often recalled to me a letter he had received from a close boyhood friend who had read in the papers of my father's activities. He wrote: "Judas betrayed a Man, Benedict Arnold betrayed a nation, and you, my friend, have betrayed a race!" A white intruder from the North, or a black man staging a rebellion—that was almost to be expected. It had already sullied the ways of the Old South after the Civil War. But my father embodied the Old South. And for him to sell out his own people could elicit the rawest rage. Twenty years after these events my father still knew that betrayal letter by heart. And he could still quote his reply. "I have full respect for your sincerity and integrity and hope that at some time in the future we may renew the ties which were so strong between your family and mine in days gone by. . . . May God's richest blessing rest on you now and always."[16]

One morning Charles C. Walker, a black minister who lived down the street, came to my mother and warned her to get my brothers out of the front bedroom of my parents' home. The house stood about forty feet back from the sidewalk. "Don't let anyone sleep in there. It faces on Chester Street. It's dangerous. People are threatening bomb throwing and acid throwing. People drive by at night with rocks and guns." My mother moved David and Jonathan to a back bedroom. Jonathan still remembers vividly how my father instructed him on what to do in case of fire. The box of valuable family papers sat on the floor in the front bedroom, hidden in a closet. If fire broke out and Jonathan was at home, he was to pull the box from under the hanging clothes, slide it out—it was on the waxed wood floor, not on a rug—and race out of the house with it. "Stop for nothing else. Just the box. Grab it and run."

My mother had already received several telephone threats of acid throwing—at her and my younger brothers. People would fill a water pistol with battery acid and shoot for the face. She was not a fearful woman, but with those threats she took precautions. She would watch carefully, she said, when she left the house, exercising particular vigilance with my brothers, never walking alone into a grocery store and never going out alone at night.

Throughout the 1957–1958 school year, cars with black men would station themselves slightly down the street from my parents' home, all during the night. At first my parents feared attack from them, but they were there to guard my family *against* attack. Ironically, they were also keeping an eye on what my father discovered as "a car parked near our home every day . . . occupied by Governor Faubus's

1863 Chester Street, Little Rock, the Ogden home, 1954–1958.

policemen." In addition, my mother soon realized that each night black men hid in the hedges and shrubbery near my parents' house, also to protect our family. By the year's end witnesses were saying, "Those closest to [my father] grow tense in concern for his safety."[17] We never did learn who had sent the protectors, but in later years my mother said she suspected that the Rev. Charles C. Walker was the guardian angel.

The fear of violence my parents shared with the Bateses equaled their fear of the anticommunist witch hunt. McCarthyism had spread everywhere. Blacks and Jews were suspected of subversive activity. Support of an aggressive integrationist could be viewed as an attempt to overthrow the American way of life. In their *State Press,* L. C. and Daisy Bates reprinted an unsigned editorial from the *Washington Post,* "What Goes on Here?" Mississippi's senior senator, James Eastland, is exploring "alleged Communist influence in the Southern Conference Educational Fund. . . . Now Senator Jenner is conducting a hearing in Memphis. Mr. Jenner seems to think, like Mr. Eastland, that ordinary Christian kindness, if it is exhibited by a white person to a colored person, is Communist." Republican Jenner (of Indiana) chaired the Senate Internal Security Subcommittee, with Eastland its ranking Democrat. The white person with her act of "ordinary Christian kindness" was Grace Lorch, who had sat with Elizabeth Eckford at the bus stop on Integration Day. Now, two months later, Mrs. Lorch was being subpoenaed to appear before the Internal Security Subcommittee of the U.S. Senate.

"Common knowledge" held that the NAACP was a Communist organization, as were supposedly the Southern Conference Educational Fund and Martin Luther King's Southern Christian Leadership Conference. According to recently released FBI files, in J. Edgar Hoover's mind these "agitators" and "troublemakers" stirred up chaos toward anarchy and then some kind of Communist takeover. The Bateses fought an ongoing anticommunist harassment battle. Their editorials steadily beat the drum of the American truth versus the American shame of the Little Rock crisis.

My father feared that he would be called before McCarthy's House Un-American Activities Committee or the Senate Internal Security Subcommittee. At the same time, he harbored a daring feeling that if they did give him a table and a microphone, he'd have a major pulpit from which to be heard by many.

My parents knew their telephones were tapped. Two agencies were listening in on the Ogdens' and the Bateses' telephone calls: the FBI and Orval Faubus's Criminal Investigation Division (CID) of the Arkansas State Police. The FBI and CID were also recording license plates of cars close to the Bates home and at gatherings such as my father's Thursday Group for the parents of the Little Rock Nine. The license plate numbers are now a matter of public record in the archives of the University of Arkansas Library. No one who has not lived through that era can sense fully the disease of fear spawned and spread by McCarthyism—its virulence and its high degree of contagion.[18]

In December 1957 the Arkansas Legislative Council authorized the state attorney general to hold public hearings, reported the *State Press*, "to determine if the Communist Party is responsible for the 'racial unrest' in the state." The NAACP had been branded as a haven of Communists and left-wingers. Most black teachers were or had been affiliated with the NAACP. If the organization was indeed subversive, they were subject to firing. A warrant was issued for Daisy Bates's arrest as NAACP president. She presented herself. She stood her ground, repeatedly refusing to give names of NAACP members. In the end she was fined $100 in Little Rock municipal court for failing to comply with the ordinance.[19]

At Central High the Mothers League began protesting in response to rumored information that one of the Nine, Minnijean Brown, would sing "Tammy" on the annual Central High talent program. The *State Press,* as well as the *Gazette,* carried the story. One of the Mothers League leaders, Mrs. Margaret Jackson, "operates a grocery store in the heart of the Negro community and with almost exclusive Negro patronage," wrote the Bateses. They went on to report that Vice Principal Huckaby immediately responded that the deadline for applying to appear on the program had passed "and no Negro students have applied." Apparently Minnijean had said to fellow students and to Vice Principal Huckaby that she intended to try out to sing on the talent program. From other reports it is unclear whether she missed an application deadline. In any case, school officials did not permit her to sing her "Tammy." The denial of Minnijean foretold the explosions she would ignite. My father and the Bateses would become involved.

Music played a key role in the family and church life of the Nine. Four of them had pianos in their homes. At the close of the 1957–1958 school year, the Central High School yearbook would picture Minnijean as a member of the Glee Club, but it was a fabrication. In choosing to go to Central High instead of Horace Mann High, the Nine had surrendered their right to participate in extracurricular organizations.

My father's influence spread not only through his preaching. Because of his daily habit of going out and visiting people in their homes, nursing homes, and hospitals, he stayed in touch with the black community as well as the white community. He would take magazines and the Sunday newspaper to the black wards in local hospitals. He was loved and respected for the amount of visiting that he did in the homes of members of his congregation. In these personal, daily conversations and frequent prayers with his people, in two or three dozen church meetings each week, and in his sermons from the pulpit he was trying to hold his congregation together. At times in a sermon he would also reveal his own private searchings. On November 3, he preached on "The Will of God for Your Life." On November 10 he asked, "Why Obey God?" He said to his congregation, "There is *NO such* thing as *altogether pure* motive. *No such thing* as completely *altruistic* behavior as long as we are imperfect human beings. Even the martyr is getting a certain satisfaction out of carrying through the thing he feels is ideal and meets with the *approval* of those whose approval he values most. Recently a minister was talking with some friends and said 'I have the approval of my fellow ministers.' When one does a deed which he himself recognizes to be *Noble*, this inevitably builds up his *self-esteem* and his idea of prestige in the sight of *men* and *angels* and *God*" [his emphasis in his notes].

My father was looking deeply into his own heart, returning always to the foundation of his theology. The two messages—"The Will of God for Your Life" and "Why Obey God?"—encapsulated his own private theology that God wills a plan for each individual life and that each person should seek to discover God's will for his or her life and obey it. My father had said repeatedly that on Integration Day, September 4, standing with the black students about to approach Central High, all at once he knew that "this is the will of God." A man given to lifelong questioning of the most serious tenets of the Christian faith, given at times to doubts so heretical that he could never share them with any parishioner or fellow pastor, my father needed certainty, and he was surprised that morning when it came.

At the end of November, President Eisenhower withdrew the last of the 101st Airborne Division, leaving the federalized National Guardsmen in charge, most of them Arkansas men and boys. The Bateses wrote a front-page editorial about anger. "The Negro is angry because he is watching his children being spat at, pushed, knocked down, 'cussed,' and made victims of all kinds of insults and abuses at the hands of those whom he thought were fellow Americans." They went on: "The Negro is mad because those whites who are ashamed, confused, and afraid, don't have the courage to stand up to their conviction and tell the few whites who are happy where they and their leader [Faubus] is taking the name of our once fair city." It was Thanksgiving. "The Negro," wrote the Bateses, "has little to be thankful for."

My father drove his car to several dozen homes in poor sections of town, delivering to each household, some white and some black, a grocery bag with a Thanksgiving turkey and other food, as had been his custom since Staunton days, walking with the bag up to each house or apartment door, ringing the bell, saying to each family, "We want to bring you a little Thanksgiving." It was something he did personally, usually alone—taking us boys along when we'd go—on his own initiative, using some church discretionary funds.

"Thank you, Reverend Ogden. We wish you a happy Thanksgiving," they'd say. There were always ragged shirts, mouths with front teeth missing, somebody wiping her hands on her apron, an old person leaning on a porch post to balance a blown hip socket, yellow eyes, a middle-aged man whose muscles had lost their tone flipping an ash from his cigarette, a kid with a jaw-breaker candy. All of them a light year away from my father's congregation. Such is my child's memory. Perhaps viewed in hindsight, my father in this role may come off as a "Lord Bountiful." Was there a patronizing attitude in him? Was there condescension? How can I look into his heart and tell? But as I look back, I see many times when he went far out of his way to give somebody a hand, when I'd watch him drained from exhaustion going out the door to make one more visit, when he'd invite ragged, smelly people off the street into the church, much to the visible and vocal discomfort of members of his congregation.

It was while searching for appropriate Christmas Scripture that my father found his prophetic voice. He rediscovered the might of Malachi, the last Old Testament prophet. When my father declaimed Malachi, he chastised with the voice of an angry prophet. On Sunday, December 1, he commenced with Malachi's prediction of the coming of a Messiah: "For you who fear my name the sun of righteousness shall rise" (4:2). Malachi spoke with the voice of the Old Testament God. My father, that morning, talked to his people about "Great Expectations."

Having opened the Book of Malachi, my father hit his stride on the following Sunday. His sermon title, "Questions before Christmas," does not reveal the vehemence of Malachi's thunder: "You have wearied the Lord (Jehovah) with your words. Yet you say, 'How have we wearied him?' By saying, 'Everyone who does evil is good in the sight of the Lord, and he delights in them.' Or by asking, 'Where is the God of justice?' " (2:17). In the mouth of Malachi sat the mouth of

God. He exhorted with the tone of an impatient God. He chastised with the cry of an angry God. When my father declaimed Malachi, he could speak with a directness and passion that contradicted all his seminary training in producing a respectable Sunday sermon. Long ago my father had switched from the word "sermon" to the word "message," from admonition to news. Now, coming in from the city streets and council sessions, he could loose the thunder of the mighty lines of Malachi.

In Malachi, my father found ten questions asked by self-righteous hypocrites of the ancient prophet's day, and on December 8, he declared to his Little Rock congregation that all people need to answer those questions in order to purify their attitudes before entering into the Christmas season. "Have you been cynical," asked my father, "because you have not received exactly what you want, and have you used this as an excuse for refusing to do God's will?"

The theme of discovering and then fulfilling God's purpose for one's life runs through many of my father's sermons. Here my father seems to link an individual's free will with God's fixed design for each life, the Calvinistic notion of "predestination." At the farther range, he told his congregation that "God has a plan for every man and he has a plan for men." If one turns to God and truly finds His will, then purpose and direction will govern each hour of each day instead of drifting, aimless and without direction. The image of shipwreck in life recurs in my father's sermons. After drifting in a sea of depression, he had found in Little Rock his direction.

Standing out there at Central High School on September 4, 1957, my father had come to know God's plan for his own life. He had seen God's will for racial justice. Now three months later the opposition raged all around him. There in his church on that pre-Christmas Sunday, several dozen of his own congregation sat tight-jawed in disagreement, some even turned their heads away as he preached, while another several dozen boycotted the worship service altogether. My father was pressing to measure up to the task as he saw it. And Malachi was giving him his lines.

Worse than the waning of the supportive spirit in the white community, the Bateses saw the black community as apathetic, and they said so over and over again in their editorials. Eventually they would blame the bankruptcy of their *State Press* on a segregationist boycott of their ads and on the "apathy of the Arkansas Negroes toward the

Thanksgiving dinner, 1957, with the Nine in the home of Daisy and L. C. Bates (at far left of photo). Clockwise from Daisy Bates: Jefferson Thomas, Elizabeth Eckford, Ernest Green, Minnijean Brown, an unidentified NAACP official, Gloria Ray, Carlotta Walls, Terrence Roberts, Melba Pattillo, and Thelma Mothershed. (Photograph by Will Counts.)

stand the paper has taken in the integration controversy." In their edition of the *State Press* right after Integration Day, the Bateses wrote: "The shocking but not surprising action of Governor Faubus Monday night, in using troops to resist the law, should incite every Negro in Arkansas to concerted action." It did not.

The Bateses saw the black church as the center of the black community. At the end of November 1957 they ran an article that announced: "NAACP Charts New Program to Win Church Support for Civil Rights." At the national level, the NAACP, with Daisy Bates at its head in Arkansas, was setting about "to mobilize the support of organized [black] religious groups in the current civil rights struggle." The four objectives of the NAACP were to get out the black vote, to create links between black and white churches, "to emphasize citizenship rights during services," and to increase participation in the NAACP.

The upheaval also changed the voice of the Bateses. From September 4 on, they featured the Nine every week on the front page of their newspaper. During the 1957–1958 school year, one third of all *State Press* issues printed a front-page photograph of the Nine. By November the paper was referring to Daisy Bates as their "mentor." At Thanksgiving, they were seen sitting around the Bateses' dinner table. Her public talks were reported, all over Arkansas and eventually all over the country, first to NAACP groups and then to white and interracial organizations.

Not only did the Bateses wish to keep the Nine in front of their readership, they wanted to shake up the black community. "It is time for the Negro mass to do its own thinking and stop being misled by professional exploiters," they had written on the front page of their *State Press* that September. Right off they blamed black voters for the election of Faubus. "The day of vote selling has passed. . . . It is unfortunate that Negroes put Faubus in office." Now in December the Bateses were publishing a front-page editorial about blacks trying to persuade parents of the Nine to withdraw their children from Central High. "You're wasting your time," they wrote. "No parent is going to jeopardize the life of his child; subject his child to insults; have his child called names, spat on and made targets for inhumanity to win constitutional rights, and then submit just when the battle is about won."

Then came the blow. The Christmas issue of the *State Press* featured the headline "Suspended . . . ," and laid out the story. "Minnijean Brown . . . was suspended Tuesday for an indefinite period."

> Minni is accused of spilling chili on a white student. Ordinarily, it is reported, such an incident would easily be erased with the familiar "excuse me," but circumstances surrounding this one made a suspension inevitable.

From here on into the spring of 1958 the *State Press* would focus no less than two dozen articles on Minnijean, the "bad girl" among the Nine—and my father would come to her defense.

3

"I didn't know it could cut so deep."

Spring 1958

On Valentine's Day 1958, the *State Press* announced that Minnijean had been suspended for a second time. School Superintendent Virgil Blossom called a press conference at which he reported the incident. The white boy had spilled hot soup on Minnijean, she had "got him back," and now a white girl had thrown a purse and hit her with it, calling her "you nigger bitch." Minnijean told the *State Press*, "I didn't know it could cut so deep." She had shouted back, calling the girl "poor white trash," thus violating the Nine's strict nonretaliation instruction. The *State Press* reprinted an editorial from the *New York Herald Tribune* remembering Branch Rickey's admonition to Jackie Robinson when he hired Robinson to play for the Brooklyn Dodgers. Rickey told Robinson, the first black in all-white professional baseball, "I want a man with guts enough not to retaliate." The *Tribune* editorial writer felt that that was a bit too much to ask of a teenage black girl under the Central High circumstances.

Three weeks earlier a student, Richard Boehler, had attacked her physically on the school grounds. It was vicious. Minnijean's mother had witnessed the assault. (Boehler was the nephew of none other than the missionary to the Congo from my father's church. Such ironies mark every turn in this black-white saga.) My father brought Minnijean's family pastor, Boehler's pastor, and another black clergyman to our home in order to take personal action. They then went to parents, and my father directly to Virgil Blossom about the Boehler incident. He had already met Blossom in Fayetteville, Arkansas, before Blossom had come to Little Rock as superintendent of schools. According to my father, Blossom and he had "remained good friends" throughout the controversy.[1]

Where Elizabeth Eckford held it all in, Minnijean Brown let it all out. The classic photograph of Elizabeth shows a thin, demure, innocent fifteen-year-old, shy eyes behind sunglasses fixed on the street ahead. She walks along in front of Central High clutching her books to her, surrounded by an angry mob of adults and students. The classic photograph of Minnijean (pronounced Minnuh-*jean*) in fall 1957 shows a broad-shouldered, athletic, brash, flirtatious sixteen-year-old on the Central High campus. She looks a white boy straight in the eye, her head cocked in a teasing laugh, her right hand flopping forward, shooing him off with a mocking "Who do you think you are?" gesture. She stands as tall as he. He has his hands on his hips. Two other white boys seem interested, one with a pencil tucked behind his ear. They form part of a crowd. None of the other Nine are there. Dozens of boys and girls mill around under an oak tree, chatting with each other, laughing, paying no attention to Minnijean, waiting—all fresh-scrubbed, clean-cut kids in jeans and light, collared shirts, and ironed blouses and dresses. They have exited the school temporarily because of a bomb scare. Helmeted paratroopers line the sidewalk behind them.

After the chili dumping, this purse bashing and "white trash" incident constituted Minnijean's second offense. School Principal Jess Matthews nailed up the notice: Minnijean Brown had been let back in "with the agreement that she would not retaliate verbally or physically to any harassment." Now she had "talked back." That did it. Both Blossom and Matthews agreed that "the suspension is expected to be permanent."[2]

Expulsion was up to the school board. The school board refused to grant Minnijean's parents, Mr. and Mrs. W. B. Brown, a hearing with their attorney present. Roy Wilkins, national executive secretary of the NAACP, sent a telegram to the board: "Your records will show that the New York office of the NAACP has refrained from injecting itself into the Little Rock situation." This time he requested that the board "reject the recommended suspension."

More people and more tension filled the next Thursday Group meeting than at any time before. Afterward my father confided in black pastor C. C. Walker that he regarded Minnijean as "the most high-spirited of the Negro children. She is a leader type. And it is more difficult for her than for any of the others to adjust to the atmosphere." At that point my father tried to intervene. It was his second direct insertion into the Minnijean hostilities. He knew personally not only Superintendent Blossom but also several other members of the school board. Now with the threatened expulsion of Minnijean my father went directly to the board, as a private citizen and in the name of the Little Rock Ministerial Association. In his plea for Minnijean he focused on what he called "extenuating circumstances, specifically the use of a mere technicality under pressure from so many people who want to get every last living one of those nine children out of there." But he failed to persuade the board. They threw her out.

On February 21, the *State Press* published on its front page a photocopy of Minnijean's suspension notice under the headline, "Bias School Board Members Expel Negro Girl." It was accompanied by an editorial by A. M. Judge, who wrote, "The expulsion is one of the most daring displays of prejudice ever perpetrated by the so-called white intelligentsia against a Negro. . . . This betrayal is enough to make any teenager lose faith not only in democracy but God as well." (Some suspected A. M. Judge was a pseudonym for the Bateses, more specifically L. C. Bates.)

On February 28, the *State Press* announced in a front-page headline, "Minnijean Enters N.Y. School." Expelled on a Friday, she enrolled the following Monday in the New Lincoln High School, an experimental, interracial school operating under the auspices of Columbia Teachers College in New York City. She went to live in the home of Professor and Mrs. Kenneth Clark and their two children, he a faculty member in anthropology at City College of New York and a trustee of New Lincoln. The whole arrangement had been engineered, together with a $1,040 scholarship for Minnijean, by the principal of New Lincoln and its board president. They were white. The Clarks were black. They had all monitored closely the situation at Central High and had followed each detail of Minnijean's story so that when the moment came, they were ready to move. At the Little Rock airport, the remaining Eight and a hundred well-wishers said their good-byes to Minnijean. Minnijean's mother accompanied her on the flight. A bomb threat delayed takeoff.

Shortly thereafter my father and mother visited Minnijean in New York, together with Roy Wilkins (NAACP executive secretary) and Gloster Current (NAACP director of branches). "I remember walking down the street," said my mother, "your father and Minnijean behind, and here was one black man on my right and another black man on my left, and here I am a white woman, and I kept thinking what are people going to say—you see, I couldn't have done this in Little Rock."

Meanwhile, back home, Governor Faubus, his eye on a seat in the U.S. Senate, told the papers, "If Minnijean Brown can go to New York, I don't see why I can't go to Washington."

Over at Central High, two white students, Sammie Dean Parker and Richard Boehler, were suspended for their involvement in hate incidents. Sammie Dean was distributing cards in school reading "One Down. Eight to Go." Three more Central High boys were suspended for wearing signs with that slogan on the school grounds. Their parents attempted to bring criminal charges against Superintendent Blossom for the suspension. Roy Wilkins wrote to Wilbur M. Brucker, secretary of the Army, asking that federal troops be returned to Little Rock to give the Eight some relief. He tallied forty-two reported incidents of harassment between October 2 and February 6 "in which thirty white students were the aggressors." Allowing for the Christmas recess, the incidents took place in a span of ninety school days. Vice Principal Huckaby could tally seventy-two incidents. The Guardsmen, wrote Roy Wilkins, were standing idly by, doing nothing to prevent the violence.

Though Minnijean was far away, the *State Press* continued to feature the Nine. As the black students began gathering to receive one award after another, the newspaper always inserted a separate picture of Minnijean into a group picture of the Eight. In May, with photographs of celebrations around Ernest Green's graduation, the *State Press* would include Minnijean's picture.

On Sunday, February 23, my father's message came from deep within. He reflected on the fact that one of the children for whom he had risked so much had violated his trust. Yet he could feel her rage. His own empathy and anger at her mistreatment could almost overwhelm him. She had struck back. He stood up for her publicly. His personal acquaintances on the school board had just rejected his plea. This morning, he thought, his congregation would certainly reject his message.

In the pulpit he seemed almost to be talking with himself. "Most of us have a desire for greatness of some kind," he said in his sermon entitled "Great in the Sight of God," "for outstanding achievement, for notable attainment, for recognition in superlative degree, for renown that will be lasting." The previous summer he had celebrated his fifty-fifth birthday, and he was coming to grips with the fact that in his own eyes he had not climbed to one of fame's pinnacles. Fulfilling his mother's prophecy—"You will never be able to measure up to your father"—he had not risen to his father's elevated stature in church circles. "As life goes on," he told his congregation, "we often have to modify our dreams of greatness both as to degree and direction. Some of us are *dis*-appointed. We feel that we have a rendezvous with achievement, a date with destiny, an appointment with greatness. Then we realize that we have somehow missed our appointment. This is what it means to be *dis*-appointed in some cases.

"We must ask, in considering this matter of greatness, 'In whose eyes is it important that I appear important?' In my own sight? From the viewpoint of other people? Or from God's vantage point in heaven? There is a sense in which only God's opinion counts, yet the other factors do have their place."

He closed his message: "Our master taught that to achieve true greatness *one must have certain child-like qualities* such as *humility, trust, teachableness, growth.* The really great persons have served others with compassion, idealism, concern, and constructive ministry. Consider such persons as Pasteur of France, Toyohiko Kagawa of Japan, Mahatma Gandhi of India, Dr. Albert Schweitzer, Wilfred Grenfell of Salvador, David Livingston of Africa, Florence Nightingale." Did my father have these qualities? He was asking himself.

As he often did, he carried this subject over to the following Sunday sermon. On March 2 he preached about "Opportunities of a Life Time." He said, "The life time here on earth is our *one* opportunity, so far as we know, to do something truly worthwhile. A great driving motive of my own heart has been to make this *one* life count for as much as possible" [his emphasis in his notes]. Visiting researchers Campbell and Pettigrew observed, "He *is* the voice of conscience for his colleagues no less than the city itself."[3]

This message about making "this *one* life count for as much as possible" rings a personal bell. It stays with me even today as one of the most important messages my father delivered to me as I was growing up.

Now all of a sudden he was in demand as a speaker. His own big opportunity had arrived: to amount to something beyond his own pulpit at home. In April 1958, my father flew to Oakland, California, to deliver a week of talks about "Christian Racial Relations," sponsored by the Oakland Council of Churches. He spoke at a variety of churches: High Street Presbyterian, First Congregational, Taylor Memorial Methodist; and at clubs: Rotary, Kiwanis, Men of Tomorrow; as well as to a Ministers' Breakfast and the Oakland Council of Church Women.

These trips away from Little Rock stimulated him to make strong pronouncements—stronger than those he dared in his own community. He told his California listeners repeatedly that "the black race and the white race live side by side but are separated as if by a glass partition." He got that image from seeing my brother sick with the measles in the school infirmary at Central Institute for the Deaf in St. Louis, isolated in the ward behind a glass partition. In another of his newly bold declarations he predicted that "eventually all of the races on our earth will come together. They will meld. They will intermarry. And one day we will be one, large tan race." The subject of race-mixing was strictly taboo in the pulpits of Little Rock.

Upon returning to Little Rock my father came back to Jesus. Not the sweet suffering Jesus but a Jesus he conceived as a man who took the lead role in the illustrative stories he told. Jesus, according to my father, was talking about himself when he narrated the parable of the good shepherd, the sower of good seed, the loyal son defending his father's vineyard against financial predators, and the good Samaritan lifting a mugging victim out of a ditch. "What kind of deeds did Jesus do?" asked my father. "*Kind* ones for others." Shifting his sermon style my father said to his congregation, "Jesus would *not only think* something, *believe* something and *teach* something, but he would *do* something, and that would be worth following."

He took his text for his Sunday message on the morning of April 20 from the Acts of the Apostles 10:38: "how God anointed Jesus of Nazareth with the Holy Spirit and with power; how he went about doing good and healing all that were oppressed by the devil."

My father preached that "to be a Christian is to take action." In his concern for the international implications of the racial situation, he tape-recorded a talk for the Voice of America, which was translated into twelve languages, including Russian. In reporting the Voice of America item, the *Arkansas Gazette* commented that he was "giving the 'other side' to the violence story which the Communists were so eager to repeat for propaganda advantage."[4] As the year wore on, he flew to Chicago, New York City, as well as to the San Francisco Bay Area at the invitation of various church organizations, to talk about the crisis, paralleling Daisy Bates's constant appearances across America that spring at the invitation of various integrationist organizations, including the NAACP.

At one point she and Mrs. Adolphine Terry had wanted to turn the Thursday Group into an action group and my father had dug in his heels. There were plenty of other centers for action groups. The character of the Thursday meetings differed, where frank, open discussion and prayer built emotional support for the parents of the Nine and also for other pro-integration people in the community.

At a moment in the spring when black-white antagonism reached an incendiary level, a pair of well-meaning young leaders from the Fellowship of Reconciliation, Nyack, New York, appeared at the Thursday Group meeting. James Lawson (black) and Glenn Smiley (white) had traveled to Little Rock to persuade the Nine to withdraw from Central High voluntarily as an act of peace. Daisy Bates was away. My father in fairness arranged interviews for them with the Nine, the parents, and a sampling of black and white pastors. After several sessions the pastors actually agreed to the idea or held neutral. The next day Daisy Bates flew back into town and my father briefed her. He said, "She raised the devil" the minute she heard "agreed to" and "neutral." And that was the end of that withdrawal suggestion.

Not only Daisy Bates's politics but her style antagonized many people. Through the *State Press* she and her husband always put her on display, together with the Nine. Her actions made news every week. Beyond Little Rock she received widespread acclaim. The Associated Press named her one of the Nine Outstanding Women of 1957 (together with Eleanor Roosevelt, Althea Gibson, Lucille Ball, and Queen Elizabeth II). In June the Capital Press Club in Washington, D.C., would call her "Woman of the Year."

By late spring and on through the summer the Nine were photographed with Daisy Bates as the group boarded planes to receive awards and medals for their bravery: to Chicago for the Abbott Civil Rights Award and to New York City for a similar AFL-CIO award. Plaques and medals cited their "Americanism" and their embodiment of Christian ideals. Nonetheless, vigorous dissent continued to splinter the ranks of black people everywhere. The NAACP at the national level awarded its Springarn Medal to the Nine. However, some parents of the Nine, among other NAACP members, saw to it that no additional medal was to go to Daisy Bates. Various people in the black community thought she drew too much public attention to herself. Many winced as the *State Press* chastised them for their inaction. Black clergy turned away when Bates editorials called them cowards. Several parents of the Nine felt strongly about the *State Press*'s calling her their children's "mentor."

But the pro-Bates sentiment prevailed. In an unprecedented move, the Nine rejected the medal: count her out, count us out. A month later the *State Press* was able to feature on its front page a photo of the Nine together with Daisy Bates—all about to receive the prestigious Springarn Medal—and the next week it featured a photo of everybody wearing their medals.

But at home the black community continued to conduct its particular style of passive opposition just as the white community conducted its active style. Violence was to the white community what apathy was to the black.

In May the Bateses grew even more outspoken: "The Negro in Little Rock has buried himself in a state of complacency. It was our hopeful opinion that the ministry, who reach more of the Negroes than any other segment of our people, would deviate slightly from the customary doctrine of faith in the unknown and turn to faith in the known. Preparation for the life after this has caused us to lose sight completely of the present life."

Through this time my father increasingly longed to create a church nexus for social movement. In May he found a platform from which he would influence young leaders to step forward from the black community as well as the white.

During the weekend of May 16 to 18 my father traveled to Monteagle, Tennessee, to deliver a keynote speech at the Dubose Episcopal Conference Center. The National Council of Churches and four other organizations sponsored an interracial, interdenominational conference for youth leaders and writers of materials for church young people. Their focus: the integrated schools to come. Shapers of the future attended, including Andrew Young (later U.S. representative to the UN and mayor of Atlanta), James Lawson (soon to be called "the young Martin Luther King"), and Will D. Campbell (later author of *Brother to a Dragonfly* and a dozen other books). They still talk about my father's influence on them.

"He loved to quote the Old Testament prophets, the prophet Isaiah," says Will Campbell. "I remember at Monteagle his reciting Isaiah's description of God: 'To whom then will ye liken God? . . . It is He who sitteth upon the circle of the earth, and the inhabitants thereof are as grasshoppers.' He enjoyed that image of people as grasshoppers spread out everywhere. And God could just wipe them out if He wanted to. Dunbar didn't argue points like a theologian or develop an argument, or make a case like a lawyer. He spoke with an absolute certainty. He told us how it was. With a kind of naiveté. A purity. A sort of innocence. As to integration—other churchmen said, 'It is the law of the land.' Dunbar said, 'It is the law of the Lord.' He really knew his Bible. He could argue orthodoxy with them. He was stubborn. Everything. He could cite you anything.

"We were in awe of him. He was a prophet for us. It was right after that that I went home and wrote *Race and the Renewal of the Church*. I used his Bible passages. I was under his spell."[5]

My father drove a group of white teenagers from Central High to the Monteagle conference—two girls and a boy—and as a chaperone, Mrs. Frances Parke, wife of his church treasurer. He also persuaded the Rev. Franklin Henderson to take a group of black teenagers in his car—two boys and a girl. The black students my father had gathered through the recommendation of the black Horace Mann High School's principal. The mother of one of the white girls "wants her daughter in my car," my father noted on the list of students.

Franklin Henderson was the black pastor of the Allison Memorial Presbyterian Church in Little Rock, a small black church near Central Presbyterian that my father had taken under his wing. My father had persuaded his presbytery to lend financial assistance to Allison, called a "mission church" because it could not support itself. In his Sunday church bulletin announcements, my father always called attention to events at Allison and the work there of Franklin Hen derson. Henderson regarded my father as his closest friend in ministerial ranks, black and white. When the two of them got together, something playful always emerged. When my father would walk up to a group of black pastors, Henderson could laughingly call him "the Holy Ghost."

With the integration crisis, Franklin Henderson and his wife lost many of their friends in the black community, as did the Bateses and the families of the Nine. "A lot of blacks didn't appreciate you," Mrs. Henderson told me when I visited in her home in 1997. "Did not appreciate your stepping out of the black community. There was a lot of fear. They tried to stay back. When we came out for integration, some of them weren't speaking to you." Antagonism from others turned Henderson and my father toward each other in even greater respect and loyalty. "No one called my husband 'Franklin' except your father," said Mrs. Henderson during my visit with her. "Everybody else called him 'Frank.'" When she said it, I recognized that. But when they corresponded, my father always wrote "Dear Dr. Henderson," and Henderson always wrote, "Dear Rev. Ogden." It was one of those nuances of black-white relations. To the end of his life my father always called Daisy Bates, "Mrs. Bates." Mrs. Henderson said, "My husband, he thought a lot of Dunbar Ogden. It strengthened him in his philosophy and in the community. They stuck together through trials and tribulations." Tribulation was soon to come.

When the Monteagle conference ended, my father and Henderson loaded their cars with their teenagers and headed for home. The white boy climbed into Franklin Henderson's car with his pair of black friends. At Central High he had spoken cordially to a couple of the Nine boys and had taken some blows for it. The two black girls got into my father's car with their white girl friend. In order to make the four hundred and some miles that day, they pulled out right after Sunday lunch. With them they carried piles of sandwiches and potato chips and six-packs of cold drinks because blacks would not be served in any restaurants along the way. As to restrooms, they'd keep a sharp eye out for the gas stations that also displayed a "colored only" sign. They had already spotted a few on the way to Monteagle and had noted them carefully. They sang. They ate.

They rolled along Route 64—past the small farmhouses, the fields of hay, corn, and cotton—admiring the spring that turns the farmlands of southern Tennessee so green you simply can't imagine stretches of arid ground anywhere on earth, nor conceive of people who go hungry.

Nothing buoyed my father's spirits more than a long drive and his car full of merry people. Add to that his sense of huge accomplishment. He had stood at the center of the conference. He had delivered a message of racial equality as no one else could. His insight had come hard won and shaped true by struggle in the street and in the sanctuary. Everyone looked up to him. He fought on the front lines. He spoke his mind. The bright people at the conference had comprehended, had caught the urgency, and had left determined to take action.

Franklin Henderson purred along up ahead, kids looking back and waving out of his car windows, signaling nonsense. My father taught old camp songs to his carful, some with comical words he himself had made up. "On the road to Mobile Bay-ay / Where the frying fishes splay-ay." And went through his repertoire of jokes. "Everybody point to your head. Now spell the abbreviation for mountain." And recited his comic verses as he did at home with us.

I eat my peas with honey,
I've done it all my life.
It makes the peas taste funny,
But it keeps them on the knife.

On the open road, the Henderson car slowed down. A puff of black smoke blew out of the exhaust. The Olds lurched and shimmied. Henderson pulled over, my father behind him. The Henderson car died. Henderson cranked and heard a dry "click, click." They had passed through Bolivar, Tennessee, a while back, then Somerville. By now it was late afternoon. Henderson and my father held a conference outside the cars.

"First thing," said my father, "we have to get the Negro children into your car right away, and all the white children back into my car." Henderson knew the pressure. A white driver with a black person in the car had to look like an employer transporting his domestic help. Otherwise they'd be picked up and hauled into the station house for questioning. Everyone envisioned fines and physical abuse, the girls sexually harassed. The kids rushed to switch cars without being told.

"Do you have any garage contacts on this side of Memphis? We're about forty miles from Memphis and the Arkansas border." "Contacts" meant a black-run garage or filling station.

"I do know some people in West Memphis." That was over the river in Arkansas—through Memphis and across the border. Henderson and my father watched the horizon as they talked, Henderson looking down the road to the east, my father to the west. Any sign of a black and cream car with spotlights, a Tennessee state trooper, and they both knew the roles they'd play. They did not need a rehearsal.

"Oh, no trouble here, officer." My father would do the talking. "We're just pulling over to have a bite to eat—a sandwich and some cold drinks and then we'll be on our way. We're driving to our homes in Little Rock. Yes, we're both preachers. We've been at a Christian conference. . . . Can we offer you a Dr. Pepper, officer?"

A white-run garage would overcharge a black man. If they would repair his car at all, they would delay, requiring an overnight stay. But no restaurant or motel accepted black customers. Henderson and his carload would have nowhere to eat or sleep.

My father made a quick decision. "Franklin, put your car in neutral and I'll push you." Henderson climbed into his 1957 Oldsmobile. My father got back into his light blue and white 1953 Chevrolet and crept up behind the big Olds. He smiled, remembering Henderson's chiding him about his shabby little car. "Why don't you drive a good-looking car like the rest of us preachers?" he'd say.

My father inched forward, touched their bumpers, then settled them firmly together, put the Chevy in first gear, and shoved. The cars eased up onto the asphalt. The kids held their breath, caught somewhere between terror and wonder. My father shifted into second, and they rumbled forward. Steelmen do not make bumpers nowadays they way they used to. Back then a bumper performed serious tasks.

My father thought up games with road signs as they went past. Jokes about "when push comes to shove." The kids said jittery *Wows* and *Keep it going*s. The waves in the Henderson back window fluttered spasmodically. Everybody trembled inside, on guard against a dreaded trooper. All eyes strained at the horizon line, just where the road meets the sky. A car passed the tandem pair. Did it belong to an off-duty sheriff? My father's palms stuck to the wheel, damp. Route 64 wound into Memphis. In town they'd stay off the main route until just before the bridge. My father prayed that he'd find an even-surfaced, straight slope up onto the on-ramp. Stop signs provided the largest obstacles. Henderson would brake and my father would let up. That went smoothly. But starting again up a hill or rolling down it they'd smack and release and smack again. No one had yet invented headrests, seat belts, or whiplash preventions.

Dusk. A modicum of traffic. An Esso station, a Pure Oil, then Leonard's BBQ, Krystal, and a Howard Johnson. Memphis police cars seemed to be engaged elsewhere. Some guardian angel was busying them in another quarter of town. Onto the ramp. "Mississippi River," a sign read. Banging and clattering onto the two-lane, my father's bumper rubbed up and then leveled back into the Henderson bumper. Rusty bridge struts flicked past, and beside them the clap-clap-clap shadows of rail ties. Now my father's bumper rubbed down against Henderson's and then straightened out. They sloped off the bridge.

"Welcome to Arkansas." A tightness inside my father's head let go. He put his hand at his hairline. It came away wet. He sang with the kids "The Arkansas Traveler." And then "She'll be comin' round the mountain when she comes"—for the dozenth time. Rowdier than ever, to cover the shakes. His gas gauge read a notch above E.

"West Memphis." They bumped on through. A smattering of clapboard houses gave way to house trailers, and macadam gave way to dirt off-roads. All at once Henderson's right turn signal flicked on. His side window came down. His arm stuck out and began pointing wildly over his roof to the right. Half a dozen kids' arms came out of his right-side windows, back and front, waving and pointing. My father slowed to a crawl. Henderson ground right onto some gravel. My father pushed him through the turn. And their lights caught the blue boards and corrugated aluminum siding of a building with a sign that said: "George's Garage. Leave Your Worries Here."

They did.

On May 25, 1958, graduation Sunday, my father preached on Matthew 3:47, posing the question, "What makes you as Christian different from other people?" Answering, he drew parallels between the experiences of his own life and those of Jesus's life. He said, "As a Christian you function with a deep inner calm, and you take action." He was returning to his theme of Jesus as a model, but now with more force and direct application to daily life. It was the key to a new way of preaching.

From the pulpit he talked directly about the crisis. "When I was going through the difficult days in which my life was threatened, I was asked by a newspaper reporter how I felt, and I said that I seemed to have an 'inner calm' that was not touched by the outer conflict, that I felt that my life was in God's hands."

Over at Central High it was baccalaureate Sunday—a special evening religious service held for graduating seniors prior to the graduation ceremony on Tuesday night. My father printed the announcement in his church bulletin that morning. "Let us be in prayer for those . . . at Central High School," he wrote. Toward his congregation in the worship service he reflected specifically on the events of September 1957 and their aftermath. He spoke now in terms quite different from his earlier oblique references.

The turmoil had caused an upheaval in him and had forced him out onto this path. Adversity had tested and toughened him. Through the early fall he had employed the epistle writer John to exhort his congregation as John had admonished the original church, knowing full well that a pastor cannot survive as a lone figure. In December he had seized upon Malachi and through Malachi he had found his prophetic voice.

All through the spring he kept returning to the Book of Amos, quoting in his sermons the oldest writing in the Bible, the roar and rage of a man speaking directly from the mouth of God: "So says the Lord." By mid-spring the example of Jesus the storyteller inspired in him another change in style.

He yearned for the pioneering of the first-century church. "Surely we ought to be in the vanguard as to the matter of *concern* and *ministry* for others," he told his congregation on May 25. "Are we really stirred in heart as we think of the *underprivileged,* the *disinherited*, and the *disenfranchised*?

"More than half the people in the world go to bed hungry every night and more than half the babies of this world sleep restlessly and fitfully because their mothers cannot provide them with sufficient milk, being themselves undernourished.

"We need to have a very *sensitive social conscience*, and to *lead* instead of to *lag* in ministering to others" [my father's emphases in his notes].

All through the months of April and May he had been teaching the Book of Daniel to a Central Church supper group on Wednesday evenings. Like Daniel he was reading the handwriting on the wall.

As the crisis months passed, my father must have come to know that a church congregation by its very nature could not work as the avant-garde of any social or political cause. It could not lead. A Christian congregation had to follow. And there lay a major frustration for a pastor who longed to penetrate new territory and take up social causes. He knew full well that he—there were then no women pastors in mainstream churches—he had to carry his people with him or the tie between them would unravel. My father's notes from that period and his later conversations with me show that his mind was very much on holding his congregation together and keeping the support of his "people." He was not thinking about persuading them as a body to any action in the civil rights crisis.

As to his own actions, he was not by nature an "advice-and-consent-from-the-congregation" man. He felt that a time comes when a pastor must either act or not act. No spare hours or days allow for consultation with many members of a congregation. Such had been the case the previous September 4.

Such was the case that Sunday afternoon, May 25. With pastor C. C. Walker at the black First Congregational Church he arranged a prayer service for and with the eight black students and their parents. All eight attended. (Minnijean was still in New York.) Fifty black people gathered with twenty-five white, mostly from the Thursday Group. C. C. Walker and my father summoned the Eight to come forward and stand in a unit, telling them, "We want to say a few words to you." Everyone formed a big circle and held hands, as on those Thursday mornings. They called on several ministers, black and white, to offer brief supplications. They prayed for safety, that no harm would come to Ernest Green and members of his family. They sang several hymns. At the close everybody stood in a circle around the interior of the church and they all sang together, "Blest be the tie that binds." From there most of the black group and four whites, including my father, went to the graduation at the black Horace Mann High School. That night Ernest Green and his family drove over to Central High for his baccalaureate service. So did my father, who later reported hearing "a magnificent commencement address at Horace Mann, and CHS flat compared to that."

At the supper hour of Tuesday, May 27, Daisy Bates picked up the telephone and dialed my parents' number. For the second time a call from her would imprint a pattern on their lives. My father answered. Daisy Bates said, "Dr. Martin Luther King is here in my home. I am not going to graduation. Dr. King is anxious to go, but we don't have any tickets. I understand that you do. Can you help us out?"

She did not need to mention the fact that blacks were forbidden to attend the Central High graduation ceremony that night, except for the immediate family of Ernest Green, nor that all members of the black press had been shut out of every graduation-related activity, including reporters from New York and Chicago. The city fathers feared a riot. That is why Daisy Bates was backing off from her own supreme victory moment. Ernest Green had entered as a senior, and tonight he would receive his diploma, the first black student to graduate from the first major integrated public high school in the South. He was sixteen, two years younger than most seniors. That afternoon Martin Luther King, Jr., had arrived in Little Rock, keenly aware that he was about to witness a major moment in American history.

The significance of the event did not escape my father. In the face of such events he always took immediate action—action that would involve and benefit other people. But how to gain entry to the ceremony? Each graduating senior received eight stadium tickets for members of his or her family. Eight seniors belonged to my father's church. He called up each one, asked for tickets they did not need, and, as a result, he said, "I stuffed my pockets." He then went to "a number of the black ministers with whom I supposed that I had a special tie." He offered them tickets, "enough to provide for what I felt was the black leadership of the community." Everyone turned him down. No one was prepared to take the risk.

That morning Martin Luther King, Jr., had addressed the graduating class of the Arkansas Agricultural, Mechanical, and Normal College, forty-five miles away in Pine Bluff. It was the only state-supported college for blacks in Arkansas. King had delivered a powerful, upbeat message: "This is a great time to be alive." And a challenge to the black graduates: "Many Negroes have lost faith in themselves," the same note the *State Press* had been sounding all year.

When King arrived at Daisy and L. C. Bates's home, his jail time, his Nobel Peace Prize (1964), and Bloody Sunday and the great Selma-to-Montgomery march (1965) waited in an unforeseeable future. King was twenty-nine years old, a young pastor in Montgomery, Alabama. There, on December 1, 1955, Rosa Parks had refused to get up and take a seat in the back of a public bus; the ensuing bus strike had made national headlines; and, as a result, on the morning of December 21, 1956, King had been the first black man to board the first fully integrated bus on the Montgomery City Lines. In February 1957, *Time* magazine had put him on its cover and run a laudatory feature story on him.

Perhaps when Daisy Bates telephoned my father she was thinking, as she had on September 4, that once again a respected white presence would serve to shield a black presence. Her phone call focused on a ticket for King, but by that time she knew my father quite well and what he would do. He said, "I'll come and get him."

Over at Central High, a lot of people, black as well as white, milled around Quigley Stadium. The color of the neighborhood was changing. Army transport trucks parked where streets intersected with the school grounds. A few soldiers in battle array emerged. Two uniformed policemen guarded each entrance.

My father and King were dressed each in a suit, white shirt, and tie. They stood about the same in height and weight, my father fifty-five and King twenty-nine. Without a "by your leave," my father walked King right up to the nearest gate and handed over a pair of tickets. "There was a big line behind us," said my father. "The two policemen stopped us and *reeeally* gave us a looking over." My father held his breath. And then the police waved them on into the football stadium. It was my father's impression that a photograph of King had almost never been printed in Southern publications and so the Little Rock police force did not know him by face. "Perhaps they thought he was a member of the Green family?" said my father. "They had not the least idea that Martin Luther King, Jr., had just entered the big show."

My father and King found seats and ducked quickly to blend into the audience. Bleachers ran along only one side of the football field. Dim area-floods lit the tiers, while high-wattage spotlights carved out a forty-foot-long platform down on the field.

Word was out that night that Ernest Green would not get across

Ernest Green graduates from Central High, May 1958.
(Photograph by Will Counts.)

that platform alive. FBI agents had secured upper windows of houses overlooking the stadium as possible sniper positions. "All at once the white leadership was like a horse riding with a burr under the saddle blanket," said my father.

Early in the month Ernest had done something very uncharacteristic. One afternoon he had taken Daisy Bates aside and asked "whether the police or the National Guard will be at our graduation." Was the situation heating up inside the school? She wanted to know. No, said Ernest, things had gotten ominously quiet.

But there had just been an incident. Two days earlier, after the baccalaureate service in the stadium, where Green had participated, one of the still-gowned graduating seniors—Curtis E. Stover—had leaped from a ledge and hawked and spat full in the face of a young black woman. Police Chief Eugene Smith and a fellow officer happened to be walking a few steps behind her. They arrested Stover immediately. The scene then turned into something out of the "Keystone Cops." Stover's mother arrived, picked up a wooden No Parking sign and swung at one of the arresting officers. Margaret C. Jackson arrived, fellow member and president of the hotly segregationist Mothers League of Central High School. Together with now two screaming Stover daughters, the whole lot was carted off in patrol cars to police headquarters. There Mrs. Stover fainted, Curtis tried to walk away, officers apprehended him, the sisters kicked the officers, and an ambulance pulled up. Mrs. Stover, revived, refused to climb aboard the ambulance and left with Mrs. Jackson. Court dates were set for all juvenile Stovers.

Children act out their parents' attitudes. The violent parent–violent child pattern marked many of the abusers in the halls of Central High.[6]

Eighty National Guardsmen sequestered themselves under the stands, out of sight so as not to raise the tension level even higher. Above them forty-five hundred spectators gathered to applaud the 602 graduates. Daisy Bates had told my father where the Green family would sit. He spotted them—Ernest Green's mother (a widow), his aunt, his grandfather, his brother, and a neighbor—a small handful clustered in the front row, to the left, just behind the parapet at the south end of the stadium. King did too. "Shall we sit with the Greens?" he asked.

My father stayed motionless. That was asking too much. Then he saw two seats just behind the family. He was the host, they had come this far, King embodied monumental courage. My father thought, "Nobody knows who in the world King is. And few will recognize me." He said, "Yes." The two of them got up and descended and sat, "acting completely naturally like you *know* you're right, not sneaking down there and not acting like a big shot." My father leaned over to Mrs. Green: "May I say to you that Dr. Martin Luther King has come here so that he may have the pleasure of sharing your experience and seeing your son graduate. This *is* Dr. Martin Luther King. This is Mrs. Green—and Ernest Green's family." On formal occasions my father could adopt a stately Edwardian tone.

Up on the platform sat the dignitaries: School Superintendent Blossom, Central High Principal Matthews. Beside them, tables with stacks of diplomas. Audience and seniors sang "America the Beautiful." A Methodist minister, father of one of the graduates, prayed. Then four-and-a-half dozen students presented a student-composed choral reading entitled, "The Story of Arkansas," with background music by the Central High Choral Department and Concert Band. One set of verses recalled,

> *Negroes, slaves to old King Cotton,*
> *Toiled beneath the broiling sun,*
> *While their masters lived in leisure,*
> *Heeding not impending doom.*

The impending doom was the Civil War. The hundred-line recital finished with the thought that

> *Through the dreams, courage, and efforts of Arkansas youth of today,*
> *Greater factories, museums, better schools, utilized resources*
> *would mark tomorrow's Arkansas.*

The moment came. The graduates, boys in blue gowns and girls in white gowns, with their mortarboards balanced on their heads, rose and stood to the left of the platform. All pregraduation photographs without exception show Green somber in his gown standing by himself a few yards away from a convivial collection of white classmates getting ready to celebrate. Two days earlier he had walked alone, without the customary partner, at Sunday's baccalaureate service. For tonight's ceremony Green's chair had been slid aside several inches so his graduating neighbor would not have to sit too close to him.

Each name was called out by a presiding school board member. First a row of girls. Then a row of boys. The student climbed the steps, emerged suddenly into the spotlight, into a burst of applause and cheers, crossed, shook hands with Principal Jess Matthews, clutched a diploma from the principal's reach, moved right, descended at the far end, and disappeared back into the blue-and-white throng. "Samuel Langford Gill, David Paul Gjestvang, Clifford Mark Goodson, John Morris Goodson, Jerry Edward Goshien."

"Ernest G. Green." The call out rang. A packed Little Rock stadium had never heard that kind of silence. The audience sat mute in its framework of semidarkness. The Guardsmen underneath them leaned forward, held their rifles. Green stepped up into the edge of the light—one more out of the endless row of caps and gowns, one more clean-cut young man, "G" in the alphabet, number 203—and strode in almost rehearsed step across the platform, shook hands, grasped his diploma in his left hand, one more high school graduate tonight, and, to the fading of nervous applause and a few taunting whistles, he was gone.

Many diplomas later the Methodist prayed again. The band struck up and everyone stood and sang Central High's school song.

> *Hail to the Old Gold!*
> *Hail to the Black!*
> *Hail Alma Mater,*
> *Naught does she lack.*

And the festivity finished. Green joined his family, and with King and my father they started moving toward a far gate where three police cruisers waited to escort their cars over to the Bateses' home. All the bad publicity had laid a plague over the local business community, and, according to my father, "The city of Little Rock wanted to show that they could go through this without having a full-fledged riot."

The Green family group continued to make its way, my father walking beside King, his hand under his elbow, assuming that he would continue to chauffeur King. The next instant a white policeman sprang out of the crowd and grabbed my father by the arm. "What are you doin' here with this bunch of *niggers*?" he said. "You know better than that. You know white people are supposed to go out *those* gates. There's a gate over there for these people. Now, you *go* where you belong."

My father said that the policeman yanked him away from the Green family "and then he just *slung* me around. I just spun, 365 degrees. And I felt for the first time, I think, in my life what a horrible thing it is to be physically mistreated when you don't deserve it, and it is the law, the representative of the *law* who is treating you in an unlawful way."

He rushed back to his own car, drove home to pick up my mother, went and got a retired white faculty member from the local black college, Philander Smith, and rounded up half a dozen black and white people to whom the party with King "would *really* mean a lot."

Martin Luther King, Jr., congratulates Ernest Green upon graduation from Central High, Little Rock, May 27, 1958, with Daisy Bates. Ogden had brought King to the graduation ceremonies. (Printed in *Jet*, June 12, 1958.)

Whenever an earth-shaking event occurred near my father or a significant person crossed his path, he would scoop up as many people as he thought would profit from the moment and enjoy it. Instinctively he responded to every major occasion with, "Who else?"

Over at the Bates house, my father's group filled out a crowd of twenty or thirty on chairs and ottomans and footstools gathered around King in a big armchair. All the black adult participants in the

Duct-taped picture window, held together by chicken wire, in the Little Rock home of Daisy and L. C. Bates, 1957 or 1958. Daisy Bates at far right. The window was the target of drive-by shooting and rock throwing. (Printed in *Life*, September 22, 1958, courtesy of Getty Images.)

integration of Central High were there, including parents of the Nine. Downstairs in the basement two dozen black boys and girls, including the Nine, played records and danced. Minnijean had flown back from New York to join in.

Tape crisscrossed the plate-glass picture window in the living room, and a web of chicken wire held it in place. No one sat near it. During the school year it had been smashed by rocks and shot out fourteen times. The Bateses kept count. In their *State Press* they called their home a house in a war zone. Three times the Ku Klux Klan had burned crosses on their lawn. People would sneak around to splinter out a back window with an acid-filled bottle. Four incendiary bombs had hit. During tense times in town, L. C. and Daisy Bates, together with the Reverend Luther Jeffries from across the street, would spell each other sitting shotgun through the night. Mrs. Jeffries still recalls a night when L. C. and her husband climbed along the roof with a garden hose to put out a fire from a Molotov cocktail—drive-bys would pitch them—while Daisy Bates sat out front with the shotgun.

My father told me, "I remember special meetings were held in the Bates home, meetings of little groups around in the community. There was a great deal of interest in this school integration. Everybody focused on it, in his or her own way. We were having a meeting one afternoon in Mrs. Bates's home and just then—maybe a dozen of us, discussing some phase of this long, continuing problem—a car went by and looking out through this window we saw someone throw an object which was about this long [*his hands spread twelve inches*] and about this big around [*his hands formed a three-inch circle*]. The car went by fairly rapidly. The object landed in the carport.

"Someone shouted, 'My God, it's a stick of dynamite.' We all jumped up and ran to the back of the room—through to a back bedroom. We ran back there, waiting. We waited, waited, and it didn't explode. Then Daisy Bates's husband stepped very cautiously after we'd waited for quite a while—he left and got a shovel. He crept through the kitchen and out, and looked at it, and called to us, 'It's the *newspaper*.'"

King was spending the night as the Bateses' guest. "Everything was on the qui vive there, in that home," said my father. A drive-by shooting could occur at any moment. "They could have driven past. They didn't know who Martin Luther King was. But even if they had—it was evidently a celebration: the most hated woman in town, you see, and the most hated woman's husband in town. But we just followed their lead, which was: They conducted their lives in a way they had a *right* to."

The next morning my father took King to the airport. Daisy Bates as King's chauffeur would have led to unpleasantness. They drove out there early for breakfast. The airport was the only place in town where both white and black people could eat commercially—because it was under control of the United States government. My father invited a black Congregational minister along, Charles C. Walker, "whom I greatly admired and was about my age."

He also called up Bill Shelton, assistant city editor of the *Arkansas Gazette*. Shelton was a member of my father's church. His boss on the paper was Harry Ashmore. My father thought that Ashmore "wrote some very good editorials." Ashmore and the *Gazette*, both editorial writer and paper, in an unprecedented moment would win Pulitzer prizes in 1958 for integration coverage. "But they wouldn't go as far as I wanted them to," said my father. "They went almost up to the point of saying: 'the time has now come, and we should.' So near."

My father phoned Shelton because no one among the white journalists was paying any attention to King's presence in Little Rock. He told Shelton, "I want to invite you to come as my guest and sit at the table with Mr. Walker and Dr. King and myself—and let us just sort of give over to you and Dr. King, and you ask him as many questions as you want to, and get yourself an interview."

Shelton asked, "Do you think this is a suitable place? Don't you think it will be inviting trouble?" It did. When King, Walker, and my father opened the door of the airport restaurant, over in the corner sat none other than Mr. I. E. Jones, a member of my father's church who night after night had plagued my parents with hour-long telephone calls, and had even offered to pay their moving costs if they'd "get out of town." My father did not know Jones by sight, but through breakfast out of the corner of his eye he kept seeing the man staring at them: fixed, riveted, never taking a sip of his coffee, menacing. That look in his face, was he sane? Was he carrying a weapon? Would he do them any harm? King and Walker sat with their backs to him. My father chatted amicably, animated as usual, while his innards ground with dread and indecision. He watched King's eyes and, beyond him, Jones's. Should he make a move to protect King? My father's premonitions would meet tragic justification. Four months later a woman would emerge from a New York crowd and stab King. My parents, coincidentally in New York, would rush to his hospital bedside. A decade later a man would emerge from a Memphis crowd with a high-powered rifle and gun King down.

Eventually Shelton did put in an appearance at the airport for a few minutes and then wrote "a couple of little paragraphs, as nearly nothing as it could be and still be courteous to me as his friend. I'm surprised at that. I could have called Harry Ashmore, who was his superior. But I don't think Ashmore would have come. I think so many people in the South had no idea of the significance of what had happened in Montgomery—and had no idea of the significance of what had happened in Little Rock." King boarded his flight.

Above all, I wanted to know my father's impressions of King. On the way to the airport, he had driven King by our home, introduced him to young Paul, on summer vacation from Central Institute for the Deaf, and had King say good-bye to my mother and sign our treasured autograph book. A few days before writing these lines, I found the book and King's autograph among my mother's papers. "He was like almost any other true leader," my father told me. "He was quite a gentleman. It was a pleasure to meet him. He didn't overdo his thing of saying you were so nice to come, and all, but he was quite appreciative, quite courteous."

To give someone "pleasure" with your company—that ranked at the top of my father's social assessments of other people, and "courtesy" was the sine qua non of a person of integrity.

I asked my father, "When you talked to Martin Luther King, did you feel that you were dealing with someone at the same approximate level of education, that you spoke something of the same language? You and I talked earlier about these gaps—."

My father leaped in. "No gap. I felt no gap. Not at all. You know, he had written a number of books. When you read *anything* that he writes, it shows a sign of maturity. He has a good style. No man can write like that unless he has good ideas and good education. That was borne out. He had a congenial personality, too."

About the party over at the Bateses' house after Ernest Green's graduation, my father recalled "a certain maturity in the man [Dr. King]. He seemed to know what he was talking about: This is the right way, this is the way of the future, things can't go backwards—they must go forward from this day, now that this one boy is graduated. People asked him to talk about Rosa Parks, and of course there was a lot of interest in hearing him tell that. We covered a very wide range of people asking questions. He gave other people a chance. He didn't monopolize." That someone possessed great knowledge, knew what he was talking about, and listened to others no matter how seemingly insignificant the thought or irrelevant the question—those qualities, to my father's way of thinking, marked a man of real character. I asked him whether King knew about my father's role beginning on September 4. He did, probably from Daisy and L. C. Bates. And from King my father received the all-important approval—*approval* was his word—that my father had been seeking from among his colleagues and within his own family.

Through the 1957–1958 school year one can trace the evolution of the Bateses' editorials and choices of articles in the *State Press*, from blur to sharp focus. One can also follow changes in their sensibilities, in their perceptions of the black and the white communities, and in their perceptions of themselves. Their tone changed. Their banner headline reporting the events of Integration Day, September 4, 1957, read in formal terms "U.S. Government Bows to Faubus." Two years later, in the fall of 1959, members of the black community verbally attacked black children seeking admission to Central High. The *State Press* let go a blast: "We'll say to them KEEP YOUR DAMNED MOUTH SHUT."

On May 30, immediately after Green's graduation, the Bateses reiterated: "The Negro in Little Rock has buried himself in . . . a state of complacency." They did not disguise their anger. This ongoing black apathy "disappointed" and "disturbed" them; and regarding their hope in the blacks' readiness to fight for equality, "our belief is shattered."

Meanwhile local businesses, pressured by anti-integration forces, were withdrawing their ads from the paper. The Bateses' newspaper was going on the financial rocks "due to the successful boycott sponsored by the Arkansas segregationists against the *State Press* and the apathy of the Arkansas Negroes over the stand the paper has taken in the integration controversy." But yet—and they sounded the triumphant note that would ring in history—"we were determined to see the nine Negro children complete their first year of school in an integrated school."

4

"No preacher is going to run me off from my church."

Summer 1958

My father remembered with anguish what was happening "among my people." He always called his congregation "my people."

"As the year wore on I noticed a cooling in my church," he said. "My congregation fell off about one third in attendance and the gifts to the church fell off about one third. Some of my people would sit and frown at me while I preached and would pass me without shaking hands after the service." One Sunday one of the elders waited around until the doors were closed before taking my father aside to tell him he had just received a clandestine telephone call. "Some members have telephoned almost every family in the congregation asking them to abstain from attending church and to cancel their contributions." My father winced in telling me that. Sunday morning church attendance had dropped from 125, or even 200 the previous fall, to 80 in the spring.

Throughout the whole ordeal of the integration year some people in his church took vigorous action with him. Mrs. Edith Tyra (a freelance tax consultant) attended every Thursday Group meeting with the black parents and brought food. But by the late spring of 1958 the disaffected had left the Sunday morning worship services. Quakers and Unitarians and Baha'is had started coming to fill the empty pews. It was their way of affirming integration. My father had lost whomever he was going to lose. He knew that he would not be standing there for many more Sundays. Thus released from the urgency to hold people who disagreed with him on the integration issue, and freed from the necessity of seeking the approval of others in his congregation for his own well-being and self-esteem, he spoke his true mind. At the same time, he was facing fierce opposition from beyond the bounds of his congregation. "Those closest to him," wrote Campbell and Pettigrew, "grow tense in concern for his safety."

On April 21 my father's closest ally at Central Church telephoned him, Gardner Lile. He said, "Dunbar, I have to talk with you. It's pressing. But not at the church. Can you meet me in the coffee shop of the Marion Hotel? Say, in an hour or two?" My father had never heard that tone in Lile before. Lile, a vice president of the Worthen Bank, a teacher in the Sunday School, and a Session member, had been head of the pastor-calling committee that had found my father and brought his name to the congregation for their vote of acceptance as their new pastor. "Gardner Lile, he was a prince of a man, just a good all-round man," my father told me years later.

"Dunbar," Lile said over coffee, "your days at our church are numbered. The people at our church are going to ask you to leave. That's my best judgment."

"I want you to know how much I appreciate your coming to me like this, with such frankness. How do members of the Session feel?" asked my father.

"The Session members don't sit still in their seats, and a few of the deacons are agitating among themselves behind closed doors. They want to do the Christian thing, but some of them blame you for what they worry about. You have become such a *public* figure. They're losing patience. Each incident over at Central High makes the balance shift a little more. In all fairness to you, Dunbar, I do not consider that your present situation ought to continue."

"Do you have an estimate as to about when they might make some kind of move?"

Lile drank his coffee and nodded to himself, a tall man, even when seated, with strong facial features. *He calculates with the mind of a banker*, thought my father.

"They say you are giving too much time to community efforts. Perhaps after school lets out and people start to go away on vacation," said Lile.

My father knew he had three months. And he knew church polity like the back of his hand. Legally, a congregation could not fire its pastor under the Presbyterian system of democratic representative government. Members of a Presbyterian congregation elected a ruling body of elders, called the Session. Central Church had fifteen elders, five departing each year and five newly elected each year, to serve for three years. The minister was "called"—that is, hired—by a congregation under supervision of the larger Presbyterian organization. The congregation regarded him as "the teaching elder." The second elected body, the deacons, responded to the physical needs of a church such as ushering and taking up the offering on Sunday. At the time no women were permitted to serve as elders or deacons.

Gardner Lile had gotten wind of secret meetings going on among a group of five of the deacons led by the man my mother called "the hammer." They were circularizing the congregation with anonymous printed material about miscegenation. They were developing some kind of written proposal that would squeeze my father out.

He counted daily visiting among parishioners as well as non-church members among his most sacred tasks as a pastor. He did it steadily: in private homes, nursing homes, hospitals. A month later, visiting in the home of another Session member, my father enountered another warning signal. He knocked and was ushered in by the elder and his wife. My father said, "I'm making calls out in your neighborhood this evening and I thought I'd drop by. I'm hearing some people have felt that I am giving too much time to community efforts, so I am redoubling my visiting efforts."

"I think you are too late, Mr. Ogden," she said. "I think your usefulness is over. People don't go along with their minister. They say 'No preacher is going to run me off from my church.' They feel you mix into too many things that are not affairs of the church." He said, "Sorry. . . ." She continued, "You look tired. Why don't you go on vacation? Why don't you go take six months' vacation?" The elder nodded agreement with his wife.

"Where would I get the money?"

It was her way of saying she'd like him to resign at once. He knew things were coming to a head.

On a Monday night, July 14, the elders and deacons held their monthly dinner gathering at the church. "You realize, don't you," one of the deacons had whispered to him after yesterday's church service, "this is going to be a very difficult meeting. Something difficult is going to happen. "

That Monday night each man hung a little too long on his neighbor's small talk, laughed a little too quickly at his own joke, and spun out whatever baseball observation or piece of car information he could dredge up. A stiffness marked the spasmodic bursts of male jocularity. When the meal finished, they scraped back their chairs and fell into silence.

My father stood, pulled a lectern into place, and began presiding over the business portion. He could cover his lurking angst on such occasions with his practiced formality. The chairman of the deacons opened by saying that the deacons had held a meeting and that they had decided that my father should keep records of his church hours. In general they wanted him to spend more time there. Would he also start announcing office hours.

My father said, "I'd like to ask you when was the deacons' meeting held?"

The chairman hesitated.

"Did you know you are supposed to notify me whenever an official body of the church holds a meeting?"

The conspirators waited, poised. "The hammer" took over as spokesman. No one breathed. "We had good reason to have this meeting. Our attendance has fallen off by a third and our giving has fallen off by a third. Our pews are emptying. We have to make cuts. We have to make a change right now and build back up." He drew out some sheets of paper. "Now we have here a proposal underwritten by nine deacons that on January 1st your salary will be reduced from $6,200 to $4,000 a month." A core of five and then another last-minute four had signed.   [editorial error above – should be "year" not "month"]

Finally, my father thought, *I am hearing the details. They know I can't support my family on that, and that's their way of forcing me out.* He said, "Within our church we open all proposals to the benefit of discussion."

"Hard-working, conscientious, sincere minister"—those words from various elders and deacons rang in my father's ears as the vote finally came to twenty-two against the salary-cut proposal and two for it, the two being "the hammer" and a friend of his.

These elders and deacons had awakened two of my father's demons: his huge pride and his terrible fear of poverty. When I was a boy, he could talk all through our supper about a hint of criticism that he had detected in a church member's telephone call that day or the suggestion of personal censure in the tone of voice of an elder at a church meeting.

One of the biggest fears in his life was the fear of poverty, of not having an income. It was not until the final two or three years of his life that this angst left him. It crept into almost every decision, stemming perhaps from the frugality of a childhood in a Southern pastor's family of seven children or from his own first pastorates during the depths of the depression years. Under his anxiety at a parishioner's unfriendly remark seethed the dread of "I'll be fired." When I was a child, he would often begin a conversation about money with the assurance, that "We're not going to the poorhouse." Of course, from his tone of voice I knew we were. I would see us in the poorhouse, a word that conjured a wretched, wintry scene of women and children as London street beggars in our illustrated works of Charles Dickens.

He uttered mechanically the closing prayer with his Little Rock elders and deacons at their dining tables in the Little Rock church. He heard himself say it by rote. And then he went on home, and he and my mother knelt down and prayed fervently. She was his praying companion. He drew strength from her faith and her practical nature. They struggled for the words and the words came out true, anything but mechanical. They said they held bone firm in the conviction that whatever the outcome, it would be God's will. "All things work together for good to them that love God," he intoned. "I can do all things through Christ who strengtheneth me." He often repeated those verses from St. Paul in times of trouble. He said them that night while he and my mother waited, for what they did not know. And prayed.[1]

Three days crept by. My father double-crammed his schedule full. That was his way of blotting out apprehension. Then the phone rang with the call he had expected. It was Gardner Lile. "Dunbar, the nine deacons could not carry the day. But a group of us needs to sit down with you and talk with you right away. It's critical. How about tonight?"

Gardner Lile and half a dozen elders and deacons drove over to the manse. Gardner led off. "Well, Dunbar, after our meeting last

Monday—we've never seen such a tense atmosphere—we're representing your friends in the congregation. . . ." My father listened closely but did not hear the preamble. These were the men he regarded as his "close and true friends." They cared about him. He read it in their faces. No one moved. The big window fan in the back bedroom whirred and whapped with a broken ball bearing. No air drew. The voice droned. "The majority of the congregation just cannot see eye to eye with you on this integration issue. They are not renewing their pledges and they are staying away from Sunday worship service. You know that. We love and respect you. We feel that you are doing what you think is right. We here are with you. You know that.

"Your ministry of peace and reconciliation may have been a major influence in preventing counterviolence on the part of the Negroes. You have the confidence of the Negro leaders."

Someone else said: "But you *keep on* doing things, like telling the newspapers the Negro people look upon this as an isolation ward in education, like their children are quarantined. That stirs up no end of trouble. We have to save our little church."

Lile: "This coming October we don't dare go door-to-door for the annual every-member canvass unless you are out of the pulpit. It would be a fiasco. We who love you will pledge some. But what we'd take in would be so small we couldn't run the church for the year. Last Monday night we were able to hold off the opposition, and we did vote not to cut your salary. But we have come to the hard decision that we must ask you to find a church in another city. It's not a matter of months, it's a matter of weeks."

Lile paused and glanced around the room. He had almost said the piece he had to say. He looked drained. Then back to my father, who nodded, somber. "Dunbar, we—all of us here—*we* want you to understand that if it takes you several months to find a place, we will try our best to hold the church together. But after December 31, in our best judgment that would be impossible."

Backstage Lile and Crist had persuaded the elders and deacons not to try to make a case against my father in front of the Presbytery, a larger Presbyterian governing body.

A wave of embarrassment swept over my father, that he was not "wise enough and strong enough to ride out the storm." But for the moment he kept that to himself. He did not miss a beat. The razor-sharp mind clicked in. In such situations he always took a formal tone and couched his sentences in diplomatic legalese. "Gentlemen, I understand your feelings and I am keenly aware of what has been happening in our church and in our community. I am sure that you have given this your best and most prayerful consideration."

No one sipped his coffee.

"I have a family to support. I have three boys in school. I am sure you understand our position. I will, of course, begin the process immediately, but I will not leave until I find a suitable place in a church that can pay a commensurate salary."

The minutes of the Session meetings for this period—and only for this period—have disappeared. All others survive. The published minutes of Washburn Presbytery (for October 23, 1958) are silent on the subject. Its Commission on the Minister and His Work submitted its regular report but said not a word about the events at Central Church. No subsequent report of any kind on these events has ever come to light.[2] Gardner Lile and his family stuck by my father to the very end. And when he was gone, they moved their membership to another church.

Pride and Prejudice

Bitterness and dissension hung on long in the congregation. In May 1959 my father would return to Little Rock to attend my brother Jonathan's graduation from the Arkansas School for the Deaf. He had written in advance to the interim minister at Central Church saying that he would very much like to go over to the Wednesday evening supper and worship service. The interim minister had replied, "Come. Welcome." Then a few days later a letter had arrived from the clerk of the Session: "I am sorry to say that the Session has called a meeting and directed me to write a letter distasteful to me. They voted to request you not to attend the Wednesday supper and prayer meeting." To his dying day my father would repeat that he never heard of a Session asking a former pastor to stay away from one of its church services.

What did my father do after that July night when the group of elders and deacons came to demand that he leave? Why did he not take the situation to his Presbytery? Why did he not request adjudication from the Presbytery's Commission on the Minister and His Work?

If he had done that and found no support there, he could easily have circumvented them and gone up the chain of command to his Synod of Arkansas, and right on up to the national level at the General Assembly of his church and to the National Council of Churches, ultimately laying before that interdenominational body his struggle against Governor Faubus. Why did my father not fight for his position? He had stood up publicly for the Little Rock Nine. Why did he not stand up for himself? And for his own family? Or viewed from a different angle, why did he not cash in his investment and use his national media attention toward obtaining a more prestigious church?

At home he could also have appealed to his non-Presbyterian colleagues, to his Methodist and Baptist and Congregational ministerial colleagues in the Little Rock Ministerial Association. And to his black colleagues there. Or he could have turned to the newspapers as he did almost daily in the struggle for integration.

The Presbyterian Church had officially declared itself against segregation. Nat Griswold, head of the Arkansas Council on Human Relations, wrote that my father's "views on the issue of race were rigidly logical and came in a straight line from the official position of the larger Presbyterian church. However, from the perspective of Southern orthodoxy, they were not logical but were irrational. To some members of Central Church, Mr. Ogden was a little queer, a bit 'touched.' "[3]

The Rev. Dick Hardie, a young Presbyterian minister in Little Rock at the time, knew my father well. "The people of Central Presbyterian Church would have thought Jesus was 'touched,' " he said to me. "Your father was like Jesus. He was a quiet man. He came across to the Central people as naïve. Perhaps impractical. He was what a minister should have been. He didn't surprise you. He was always with the needy. Like Kagawa."[4]

Years later I asked my father what he felt about his role as pastor to his congregation as opposed to his role in that social revolution. He said, "My interpretation of what it means to be a Christian is to have a relation as an individual to the deity, however you conceive the deity to be, and that this should result in one's doing everything that he can to help to make society what it ought to be—and that the church should be involved in all of the great social questions that have to do with equity and right living, and fairness to others, and justice. This work seemed to me to be a logical expression of my being a minister."

The Rev. William Fogleman, also a young Presbyterian minister in Little Rock in the integration period, saw the dilemma from a civic point of view. He explained to me: "Your father was a member of a class of folk. The difference was not the clerics but the laypeople, particularly laymen, men of power in the city. Your dad stood alone. He had no formidable lay allies in his congregation. 'We're not after Dunbar,' they said, 'we're just trying to save our little church.' "[5]

My father's pride drove him to the other extreme. He knew full well that only the Presbytery could dissolve his relationship with the congregation and that these elders and deacons would not want that exposed. Having been treated so crudely, he invited the entire Presbytery to hold its triannual meeting at his Central Church on September 16, 1958. With warm hospitality the women of his church prepared and served a meal to his fellow Presbyterian pastors. About to depart, he stood among them, brotherly, expansive, dignified, and articulate in his welcome as their host. A month and a week later, on October 26, at the Sunday morning worship service he announced formally to his congregation that he had accepted a call to a church in West Virginia, regretting that he was to leave them, holding them always in his prayers and love, and looking forward to the new work that the Lord had willed for his life and the life of his family.

From my earliest awareness of my father, I stored evidences of the way in which he sought to put a positive face on all episodes in his life and in his family's life. To him—dignified, organized, handsome, polite, well-informed—a fitting and appropriate public appearance revealed these inner qualities. He devoted as much care to the clothes he wore as to the words he used. Tone of voice affected him as much as the words themselves. At the supper table he could agonize over someone who had addressed him in a harsh way. Anyone who "was very discourteous" was even worse. At home, whenever he said to my brother David and me, "I am displeased by that," we shook in our shoes. Whenever he filled out a form that required a statement of health, he warned us often: Never use the word "depression" or write in something such as "heart murmur" because that would destroy any chances that one might otherwise have. In that same vein of clothing life's troubles in euphemisms, whenever my father said of a hospitalized relative, "Oh, she has just gone in for a checkup," my brother David and I would assume that she probably had cancer. In reference to money and finances, my father would tell us repeatedly, "Other people don't need to know your business." As a result, David and I behaved very cautiously with the money that we earned with our newspaper routes and working in local dry-goods stores during the Christmas and summer periods.

In every respect my father made this firing from Central Presbyterian, Little Rock, look like a positive career move. With utmost discretion he had approached a few trusted, out-of-town friends and let it be known that he was seeking another pastorate, and an old friend of the family, a minister in West Virginia, had jumped at the chance to have him as his associate minister.

It was during the final Little Rock summer that my father was struck his harshest blow while Governor Faubus pulled off the masterstroke of his career.

Back in April, a month before Ernest Green's graduation, the Little Rock School Board had entered a plea in the Federal District Court for the removal of the remaining black students from Central High and a two-and-half-year postponement of school integration. Their case: Because of the entry of the black students, chaos and tension had caused a serious disruption of the educational program, an additional financial burden had been placed on the board during the school year, and "the Board could see no prospect for improvement if integration were continued in September of 1958." In June, Federal Judge Harry Lemley decreed the suspension. The NAACP appealed. In mid-September the U.S. Supreme Court overturned the decision. Arkansas Representative Brooks Hays and Arkansas Senators William Fulbright and John McClellan all expressed regret at the reversal. McClellan predicted "irreparable harm would flow from the ruling." Senator Strom Thurmond from South Carolina denounced the ruling, saying it was "in keeping with the court's record of putting the interests of Communists and other criminals ahead of the court's duty to sustain the Constitution." Thurgood Marshall, counsel for the black students, told newsmen: "Anything now done to prevent desegregation in Arkansas is in open defiance of the law."

During late July my father traveled to New Orleans to visit his aging mother. He took a box of newspaper clippings and magazine articles with him, in order to lay out for her and several of his brothers and sisters something of his achievement in Little Rock. The oldest of seven siblings and the one of whom the most was expected, he still longed for affirmation and approval from his family. Since earliest childhood, they had shared life with black people on a daily basis. In addition, their family anecdotes included black people: the constant talk about ancestors and family traditions and antebellum days, the regard for family heirlooms. The family experiences with blacks and often patronizing attitudes toward black people, examined and unexamined, shaped the whole family's thinking.

The previous fall my father had mailed to his mother a feature article all about him from the *Arkansas Gazette*. The reporter had asked him, "Do you feel that in any way you have betrayed the Southern traditions that your ancestors helped to shape?"

"Not at all," my father had said. "I was taught that my forefathers were mainly persons of high idealism with strong humanitarian interests. I am doing my best to perpetuate the genuine traditions of the family from which I come."

His mother had never responded to the clipping.

After arriving in her home that July, he waited for the appropriate moment. Now at last he could stand shoulder to shoulder with the image of his father. When all had gathered, he got out his box, set it on the dining room table, opened it, and said, "I want to show you something." His mother reached over and closed the box and said, "Dunbar, we'll talk about that another time."

That deflection I knew in my own bones from earliest childhood. That subject in my Grandmother Ogden's household was forever taboo.

In my mind's eye, I can see my grandmother's imperious face when something unspeakable was said in her parlor. She had put on weight in her later years, and whenever someone would cajole family members into posing for a snapshot, she would always locate herself behind a short bush, her head peeping over the top, in order to hide her girth. She was four years older than my Grandfather Ogden. She could fix me with her eye whenever she made a demand, a demand she usually framed within a Bible quote. She would suck in the slightly fleshy insides of the ends of her upper lip.

After church on Sunday, when we visited in New Orleans, she never permitted us children to buy an ice cream cone—even if we had earned the nickel ourselves—because you did not spend money on Sunday in a shop, thus, according to my grandmother, encouraging other people to keep their shops open and work on the Lord's day.

I can still hear the intonation of "Dunbar." That tone I obeyed without asking why. When reproach hung in the air for me or my father, she usually addressed us as "Dunbar dearest."

They never did open that box of clippings. Two years later, my father's New Orleans brother, Warren, Sunday magazine editor of the *Times Picayune*, wrote and mailed out to all six brothers and sisters (there were seven including Warren) a typed, four-page, single-spaced, closely argued case against school integration, point for point—without mentioning my father, his older brother. He foresaw nothing less than "the destruction of a social order" in America. Go down this road, the brother wrote, "and we face the Herculean task of building a school system." That was the last my father heard. No member of his immediate family ever mentioned Little Rock to him. Their rejection cut him to the core.

A half century later one of his sisters, writing to me from Atlanta, translated the situation into genteel Southernism: "The family and I were in jobs where the repercussions of Little Rock and Dunbar's actions *did* create some 'attention' (embarrassment??), but no comment about that was surfaced." During my own childhood visits to those ancient halls, at naptime I could still hear outside my closed door the famous "Ogden whisper"—above which comment never surfaced. Fear of controversy and open dissension seems to have passed along in the family genes. That's why Grandmother Ogden had reached over and closed that box of clippings.

At the same time, a spirit of sly humor and wit always hung around the seven Ogden siblings' communiqués with each other. When my father left Little Rock to go to a church in Huntington, West Virginia, that fall, he also became the pastor of a little mission church in nearby Rome, Ohio. At the receipt of that news, his brother Warren composed and mailed off a congratulatory verse for him. During our interviews, my father could recite it to me with a twinkle, all those nineteen years later, by heart. He said it ran like this:

My brother went off from his home,
for to wander the earth and to roam.
His deeds ecclesiastical were something fantastical,
and now he's a prelate in Rome.

My father understood that with humor his brother was conquering this fear of controversy. My father himself had had to overcome it in order to bring his box of integration materials to his family. In repeating the verse he showed me that he had accepted wholeheartedly his brother's peace offering and had forgiven him. I saw the complexity of the family's way of keeping controversy at bay while staying in touch or accepting each other.

Now my father feared open dissension from his own church, from "my people." When he finished his New Orleans family visit and returned to Little Rock, he found that in Arkansas state government circles the attorney general was carrying out his "war on Communism" even more vigorously and was directing his "war against the NAACP." On September 12, 1958, Governor Faubus signed into law a state legislature bill requiring all state employees, including teachers in public schools, colleges, and universities, to disclose their past and present affiliations and to take a loyalty oath. Governor Faubus was winning a stunning victory for a third term.

Resistance often took the form of gallows humor. One of the jokes came out of the hills of northwest Arkansas, a center for opposition to Faubus. According to the story, a truck loaded with chickens on the highway from Fayetteville to Alma was tailed by a highway patrolman. At Alma the driver of the truck stopped for coffee. The patrolman pulled up beside his truck and said to the driver, "Man, you are some driver. Your speedometer stood on the maximum limit for the last ten miles, but it never went over the limit. How do you do it? Do you have a governor on your truck?"

"Oh, no sir, boss," said the driver. "It's them chickens that smell that way."[6]

Then came Faubus's coup. On the same day, September 12, he closed the four high schools in Little Rock rather than have them integrated. The Bateses again criticized the lack of support from the black community. In an editorial they wrote: "A well known [black] minister and pastor of one of Arkansas's largest churches, is quoted as saying last week that he did not endorse the crises in Little Rock, but there was nothing he could do. He said that many of his members worked domestically for wealthy white families, and he was quiet about the situation because he had to live here. It is our opinion that that should be one of the main reasons he should speak out, because he has got to live here. It is a very poor leader of people who doesn't want to better the conditions in which he and his constituents have to live."

Their editorials deplored situations where blacks were paid to try to enter white churches. "It is heartbreaking," they wrote, "to see Negroes like James Howard, an employee of Jimmy Karam, a known segregationist, carrying signs asking for integration at an all-white polling place during the recent election."

Two months after his church had demanded his resignation, my father was still exhorting his congregation to support what he thought was justice in civil rights. On Sunday, September 14, he spoke out from his pulpit about the school closing: "Some people put their Christianity aside until after a crisis is over!" He preached about characteristics of the "fellowship" of first-century Christians. "Are you a good enough Christian to have a Christ-like attitude, to have the *right* spirit toward all persons that have to do with the educational systems?"

Two days later Washburn Presbytery, twenty-five Presbyterian ministers and twenty-five lay leaders, convened at my father's church. He led them to pass a resolution and issue it to the press opposing Faubus's closing of the schools and calling on Faubus "to obey all the laws." Faubus was in New York. He had already gotten wind of the coming action. He summoned the press. When asked about this opposition to his policies, Faubus told the *New York Times* that a large number of Presbyterian ministers "have been very effectively brainwashed" by left-wingers and Communists and fellow travelers. Newspapers all over the country picked up his statement.[7] Whereas churchmen often wrung their hands over the lethargic pace of their ecclesiastical bureaucracies, Washburn Presbytery could not move fast enough to fire off a demand for redress. "In this hour of crisis, with the educational welfare of thousands of children at stake, the Governor of Arkansas has resorted to name-calling and slander." When it came to left-wingers and Communists, the matter exercised Presbyterians. "Our great church is due an apology."

Today in the archives of the Presbyterian church in Montreat, North Carolina, rests a box only to be opened publicly fifty years after it was shut in 1958. I obtained special permission. It contains passionate personal letters to Washburn Presbytery in response to this resolution, letters citing biblical passages both in favor of the integration of Central High and opposed to it. Yet even that cache of controversial materials contains no hint as to my father's firing.

On September 27 the people of Little Rock spoke with a loud and decisive voice. Faubus called for a city election to endorse his action. Passion ruled the day. With a population of 108,000, some 74 percent of the registered voters turned out, approximately 17 percent of those voting were black. They could choose between total integration and closed schools. They went to the polls and voted 19,470 to 7,561 against "immediate integration of all schools." They ratified Faubus's countermand. Daisy Bates and the NAACP lawyers moved right away to the appeals court to prevent the closing—but to no avail.

At the end of September my father went to New York City to tape an interview with CBS and a talk for the Voice of America, and to visit Martin Luther King, Jr., in Harlem Hospital. King had been stabbed. While at a signing of his new book, a deranged black woman had walked up from the crowd and shoved a letter opener into his chest. My father returned to Little Rock to preach from Isaiah and Amos, saying that the voice of the prophet is the voice of God: " 'Harken to *me*.' The '*me*' referred to is *God himself*, for the prophet Isaiah is so filled with the Spirit that he *dares to speak for the Almighty One* and to put words into His mouth." I can still imagine my father's voice calling out, "Harken to *me*," expansive and orotund like an actor in the person of Isaiah—no, not *like* an actor, he *was* an actor in that moment on the stage of his pulpit, a prophet calling out to his people.

Then from that pulpit on October 26, my father said his farewell to Central Church. In his last sermon he brought the interracial crisis directly before his congregation. A year ago September he had used his pulpit to articulate his pastoral approval of integration at Central High. He had also predicted a self-screening within his church, telling colleagues that many members who disagreed with him would leave.

His topic this October Sunday morning was "The Just Shall Live by Faith." He talked about each person's singular connection with

God, about qualities of one's everyday personal life. As on the Sunday the prior fall after he had walked with the black children, justice was on his mind.

This morning he quoted Old Testament prophets, and he thought about the will of God. He opened with Amos's rumbling poetry: "Justice shall flow down like waters and righteousness as a mighty stream." He anchored his text with Habakkuk 2:4: "He whose soul is not upright in him shall fail. But the just shall live by faith," noting that St. Paul quotes that very line in his letter to the Romans 17:1. "Habakkuk meant that here is the answer when an evil majority imposes upon a righteous minority." He set forth the need for renewed consecration of life, the truth that you have a soul that has a God, the challenge to come to God's house for worship, the essence of God's love, the need for absolute honesty, the discovery of a new beauty in life, the courage for extreme difficulty, and a concern for others.

At the bottom of his last page he finished with a story from the racial crisis. His notes are fragmentary, with a blank after "Mrs." His note "Fuller" may indicate that she was a graduate of the nondenominational Fuller Seminary in Los Angeles. The point is this. The final story that he told his congregation from his pulpit was not about his own dramatic, public experience, but about someone else's small, private moment: "The Rev. Mrs. _____ Fuller (ordained Christian minister in L.R., Ark.) told my wife and myself that for two years she had been meeting with nine negro women in L.R. one night a week (usually till midnight) reading to them and explaining every word of the Bible. When Sept. 1957 came, they never came to her house again for fear white segregationists would injure her."

That was his summing up, his good-bye: an example of personal courage in private life on the part of these women.

Years later, going through my father's detailed notes for each sermon, Sunday after Sunday, I came across this simple, modest finale: his decision to finish not with the resonant verses of an Old Testament prophet, not with a dramatic recital of events in the Little Rock crisis, but by telling in all simplicity someone else's story of quietly, almost secretly, teaching the Bible to a group of black women. I suddenly found tears in my eyes. I have quoted these lines exactly as he wrote them in his sermon notes. I have never discovered what the underscored blank stands for. The passage reveals the truest part of his nature, for with all his longings for recognition, for approval, for a central position on the world's public stage, he still and always harkened to an inner voice of overwhelming compassion, born, I think, from the pits of hell gouged by his own bouts with depression. I knew in him an abiding readiness to step into the background in the face of some profoundly good person, and I knew his obsessive, self-effacing drive for seeking the best for each of us boys and for each person with whom he came in contact. There was something instinctive about that drive, the way he would start thinking ahead with a young person, talking about college or a career choice, or working out phone calls to help a near stranger just come to town and without work, to help him find a job. As a schoolboy I overheard many of those conversations, met many of those people, often saw him jump in the car to go lend a hand.

Half a century later, as I sat reading his notes for his farewell message, I thought I could not conceive of a more vivid and accurate picture than this one: of his holding in front of his congregation the image of someone whose life went unrecognized by the world, someone who in her work embodied so much of what he wanted his life to be. And I think, on the inside, it was.

Daisy Bates describes their personal good-bye in *The Long Shadow*. She records an image of him that I never saw. "The night before Mr. and Mrs. Ogden left Little Rock for his new charge . . . they came to see me. As we talked, I noticed a remarkable physical change in Mr. Ogden's face—deepened lines on his brow, tired and sad eyes. I was reminded of his 'Calvary'—the insulting telephone calls he received night and day, the abuse and verbal indignities heaped upon his family, the rejection by his lifelong friends, and the loss of his church. This reflection of the price he had paid for decency caused me to regret having made that first telephone call to him. 'I'm sorry I got you into this,' I said.

"He was silent for a moment. Then he said, 'Don't feel sorry. If I had to do it all over again, I would.' "[8]

On October 23, just before my parents left town, the Thursday Group people held a special farewell party for them. Parents of the Nine, Daisy and L. C. Bates, the unfailing Edith Tyra from my father's church, Adolphine Terry, and other white and black people from the community came. Rabbi Ira Sanders returned in honor of my father after several months' absence.

When my parents arrived at the Dunbar Community Center, they found two dozen well-wishers gathered around something they had never seen before: a money tree. It was a small tree on a table with many dollar bills pinned to it. Elizabeth Eckford's parents and Gloria Ray's father told them that a money tree was quite common in the black community.

At the end of tributes, songs, memories, and coffee and cookies, Daisy Bates read a few of her sentiments. The first item people did not expect. Instead of focusing on heroics and the battle scarred, she reflected on a kind of forgiveness. She talked about the way my father's "Christian leadership here in the community has so influenced us that we are fast losing every vestige of bitterness towards our foes, and find it more appeasing to replace all ill feelings with sympathy for a people who could harbor such hatred, intolerance, and lack of brotherhood." From the "steely-eyed woman" who fought Faubus, who "raised the devil" at the suggestion that the Nine withdraw from Central High, and who with her husband, L. C., had already hosed out three KKK burning crosses in front of her home, those thoughts came unexpected.

Then my father made an informal little speech, some random thoughts: "We're getting more religion here than we do in our churches." He surprised himself when he heard himself say that. He went on, "This is the spiritual center of Little Rock—in the sight of God." He liked that idea, "in the sight of God."

He looked over at Daisy Bates. In May she had met with President Eisenhower in Washington, D.C. In June the Capital Press Club had called her "Woman of the Year." He said, "Mrs. Bates has been raised up of God—." Eyes brightened. You could hear a few people suck in their breath. "—to be chosen president of the NAACP. I appreciate the opportunity she has given me of counseling with her on spiritual aspects of this movement. From time to time she has asked me for material from sermons to use in some of her addresses around the country when she wanted to emphasize the moral and spiritual aspects of this crusade. Some people now say, 'Why does Mrs. Bates have to go around the country, flying from city to city, receiving armfuls of flowers, making speeches, surrounded by scores of reporters, basking in the limelight of national publicity?' I have said repeatedly, 'The leader of any really great movement has to be very much the type of person Mrs. Bates is. If she were the type of person who withered under the glare of the public spotlight, she wouldn't do for this job. I think she's very much like Mrs. Franklin Roosevelt. Such a leader has to have a sharp cutting edge, to possess an imperviousness to the resistance they encounter. They must thrive under circumstances that would destroy others.'"

At this very moment of success, surrounded by loving and admiring people, my father and Daisy Bates each had come to stand more and more alone. In the glance that passed between them, each knew that about himself or herself and about the other.

Then my father looked around the room. Faces fixed on him, expecting they weren't sure what. He said he wanted to thank them for giving him the privilege of presiding over the gatherings. "I would just like to open my heart to you. I've thought how generous you of the Negro group are in accepting my leadership. If I were in your place I'd think: Here's this white minister. Are his motives as altruistic as he'd have us believe? If I were a Negro, I would wonder if Ogden were not trying to satisfy a drive for recognition by taking the lead in this."

He confessed to gaining something from them, not just giving. "To lay everything on the line for this cause has built me up within, and given me something to live for. I do not have the feeling that I have done anything that is totally unselfish. I would hate to go away from here, your thinking that Dunbar Ogden thinks there is such a thing as complete altruism." Some nodded. Some looked a bit puzzled. Rabbi Ira Sanders got up and went over and put his arm around my father's shoulders, and said something in Yiddish. Then he explained: "In Yiddish you can call an unusual person 'a strange duck.' Well, Mr. Ogden, you *are* a strange duck.'"

That comment pleased my father enormously. Years later during our interviews, when he told me about the "strange duck" episode, he went on at some length about Rabbi Sanders's comment. He thought it was odd—a bit shocking. He liked that. I could tell from his smiles and his attention to the expression, from the way he tried to reproduce the sounds of the Yiddish words, that he thought it fit him. During our earlier interviews he had often referred to himself, with a certain pride, as "a maverick." The word "maverick" helped him to locate himself, to identify himself for himself.

5

"He taught by his actions."

Little Rock Anniversary, 1997

I am Dunbar H. Ogden, III. The third, I was named after my father and grandfather, a heavy burden laid on me in my cradle. I greatly admired both men. I honored their encyclopedic knowledge, their wisdom, their genteel ways, their profound formulations of religious thought, and their readiness to stand up for an unpopular cause they believed in and for "the downtrodden and the disadvantaged" (their words). For both father and grandfather the teachings of the Bible provided a mandate for action toward social good.

But I would not be groomed into a third-generation minister. I'd chosen "to measure up" in a different way.

In October 1956, I stood in the living room of our Chester Street house in Little Rock and said good-bye. Good-bye to life as a minister's child in a glass cage.

The whole family held hands and recited aloud what the Ogdens called "the Genesis blessing and the going away Psalm"—"The Lord watch between me and thee while we are absent one from another." "The Lord shall preserve thy going out and thy coming in. . . ." We always did that in Grandmother and Grandfather Ogden's home whenever we were leaving after a visit. (Genesis 31:49 and Psalm 121:8).

A scholarship from the German government provided boat passage across the Atlantic and a year at the University of Munich. From that point on, I was speaking German. Eventually I met and married a German girl, a fellow student. I taught in a Munich gymnasium (high school) in order to stay a second year at the University of

Munich and then taught in a Berlin gymnasium in order to spend a year at the Free University Berlin, my third German year.

I had escaped from the family. I had escaped from a father hounded by periodic bouts of depression. I had fled from the confusions of having a strong, musically gifted mother married to a sometimes collapsing and sometimes brilliantly leading husband, a man intense in his presence and, for me, demanding just by his example. Perhaps I was running away from the responsibility of two younger brothers who were deaf, from the task as oldest child of living up to the expectations of my father, the valedictorian of his class at Davidson College, where a scholarship had later paid my way. I ran from the power of a grandfather whose name I bore, he a Southern blue blood and recipient of high ecclesiastical honors. I disguised the boy who had lived in a glass cage in a community that expected in me the model of what it means to be the oldest son of the town's most distinguished clergyman. In Germany I spoke the language, read the literature, attended the theatre, wore the clothes, and ate the food of another culture. I forged a new identity.

Then one day in September 1957 I saw Little Rock on the front page of the Munich newspaper. And soon after, my mother sent local newspaper clippings, *Time* magazine, the *New York Times*—all about my father's role in the Little Rock crisis. My mother mailed the front page of the *Arkansas Democrat*, September 4, 1957, with its news photo. On it a Lt. Col. Johnson of the National Guard, nightstick in hand, was stopping several black children from entering Central High. My father stood beside them, his back to the camera. He had written on the photo, with an arrow pointing to himself, "THIS IS D.H.O. JR. YOUR DAD!" I said to myself swelling with pride, "Of course he did. That's just like him." At the next visit to my in-laws' south German home, I spread out the clippings, all of them, on their dining room table to show these people what an impressive father-in-law their daughter had in America.

The Munich newspaper, *Die Süddeutsche Zeitung*, continued to run pictures and stories from Little Rock. My German high school students knew all about it. I had been hired to teach conversational English, and I was always looking for something we could talk about. Here I found just the thing. I took the clippings from home to my advanced class and opened a discussion. They were teenagers, like the Nine. I asked for a show of hands, "How many of you would accept

Detail from the front page of the *Arkansas Democrat,* September 4, 1957, showing Dunbar H. Ogden, Jr. (back to camera, far right side of photo), with some of the Little Rock Nine. The accompanying article reported that the students "were led by a well-dressed white man in a light suit." Lt. Col. Johnson of the Arkansas National Guard stops the students in front of Central High. Left to right: David Ogden (with glasses), Lt. Col. Marion Johnson, Carlotta Walls, Jane Hill (in back, who participated September 4 but did not enroll in Central High), Gloria Ray, Ernest Green. (Photograph by Will Counts.)

a black student in this class?" All hands flew up. "Would you sit and have lunch with the black student?" All heads nodded an emphatic "Ja." "Invite him or her to come home with you?" All hands up again, with astonished *sure*s, *of course*s, and *naturally*s. Someone said, "Well, it would depend on the student's personality, who the student was, not the student's race or something like that." Then came a storm of outrage. "How could those white Americans be so *mean*?" "Why is there such a big race problem in America?" "How could white people be so violent to people different from them?" One of my students in that high school class was the grandson of the theatre director Max Reinhardt, one of many Jews who had fled the Nazis. Something made me hold off from asking the students whether they had ever had "a race problem in this country." Maybe I should have asked them. Maybe they didn't know. Their history books hadn't told them.

As I went on about my own life, immersed in studying and teaching, in Munich and then Berlin, in my new marriage, in the East-West conflict in Berlin, I remember my surprise at the continuing uproar reported in subsequent clippings from home. Despite my pride in my father, Little Rock remained geographically and emotionally remote for me. I never saw my father in action in Little Rock.

In the summer of 1997 an invitation to attend the fortieth anniversary followed me to our holiday cottage in upstate New York. I put it aside. Why should I go? But perhaps my mother would? I telephoned her in California. Maybe she needed me to shepherd her around? No, she wouldn't attempt the trip. "It would be too much," she said on the phone. (She would soon be eighty-eight.) Something in her voice—not the words (not a hint of "you should go," not at all) but the powerful immediacy of her matter-of-fact tones and cadences—conjured up heart-wrenching images of her and my father in that Little Rock house. The printed invitation in my hand and her voice in my ear suddenly called to me to do something about the interviews I had taped with my father twenty years ago and the eleven drawers of his files in my Berkeley basement.

I flew to Little Rock to pick up the story again.

Air Force One had landed. I could see it from my window as we taxied along the runway toward the Little Rock airport. I rented a car and headed for the cathedral.

The citywide Reconciliation Service was taking place at Saint Andrews Cathedral. It was packed. The Little Rock Nine, some with families, sat near the front. To the side sat Daisy Bates, now eighty-three or eighty-four, in a wheelchair. Elizabeth Eckford, carrying a candle, led the opening procession and took her place with them. Rufus King Young—pastor of the Bethel Africam Methodist Episcopal Church, now retired and age eighty-six—had been chosen to deliver the homily. He had known my father. Three of the Nine had been members of Young's church.

When his time came, Rufus King Young rose, tall, trim in a black pulpit robe, wispy white hair, glasses, a mouth used to intelligent smiling, a dignity to his face that matched his bearing and the clear, thoughtful authority of his voice. A man who telegraphed patience. He selected his text from the book of Exodus, the freeing of the children of Israel from bondage. "And the Lord said, '. . . I am come down to deliver them.'" Rufus King Young took hold of the pulpit with both hands, looked out at us, and explained in a rich Southern accent that God came down to his people in the form of Moses—and that "throughout history God has descended in the human form of Mahatma Gandhi . . . and Mother Teresa to minister to the poor . . . in the form of Nelson Mandela to deliver South Africa from the evils of apartheid . . . in the personalities of . . . Thurgood Marshall, Martin Luther King, Rosa Parks, Daisy Bates, Dunbar Ogden . . . and a whole lot of others to deliver a people from the evil clutches of racial segregation and discrimination."

My breath caught in my throat. This black minister had named my father among the most revered civil rights leaders—a white man I did not yet know: my father in Little Rock.

Next day came the main anniversary event. A red dot on the map told me where Central High stood. I drove side streets, searching from block to block for a trace of a house I might recognize. A few street names started to come back: Arch, Chester, Wright, Park. The black limousines of the presidential entourage toured along Broadway and then turned onto Daisy Lee Gatson Bates Way and crossed Martin Luther King Jr. Boulevard. I fell in behind, close to the school now. Parked cars jammed helter-skelter in the dust of sidewalkless streets. I found a slot, parked, got out. The September-morning sun stirred the long-forgotten smell of asphalt heat.

Clusters of people hurried toward the school, ringed by uniformed security guards. Guards at checkpoints passed electronic surveillance wands up and down both sides of our bodies, and in front and back. Others, pistols holstered, watched. Could it possibly occur to any of them that they might be re-enacting the September 4, 1957, encirclement of Central High by Governor Faubus's National Guard?

Handing around my briefcase, I filed through one of the inspection arches, but instead of following the crowd across Park Street toward the school, the bleachers, and the swelling turmoil, I turned and entered the Magnolia Mobil gas station. In 1957 and 1958 racists had gathered here for mob action. For this anniversary occasion the gas station with its derelict pumps had been scraped clean, painted, and dedicated as the Central High Museum and Visitors Center.

Inside hung the cool smell of a newly built home just opened for inspection by potential buyers. A polished wood-and-glass counter had replaced the finger-grimed metal desk and cash register that had long stood there, behind it a floor-to-ceiling shelf of civil rights books and Central High 1957–1997 T-shirts. Beyond, a small labyrinth of sheetrock walls and tract-house doors covered all hints of a repair garage, and a wool-and-foam-pad carpet hid wall-to-wall even the faintest trace of cement floor, lift rack, and oil pit.

Wall-sized photographs with scenes from 1957 were juxtaposed with recent scenes from 1997. I stared at an enlarged picture of the 1957 Thanksgiving dinner at the Bates home. The Little Rock Nine, all of them, are sitting around a table, heads bowed for the blessing before the meal. They look so young, so clean-cut and scrubbed. They have already been through the September ordeal of entering Central High, and the camera has caught a moment of respite from the steady abuse they are facing at school. The Bates home provided a safe haven for them. At the end of each school day they would meet in the Bates living room or den to exchange their stories, give each other strength, and take courage from Daisy Bates. At the head of the table is sitting L. C. Bates. His head is not bowed. He was not a religious man. And beside him, his wife, Daisy Bates.

Pictures from this period show Daisy Bates to be a strikingly beautiful woman. I saw how light-skinned she was. Later I learned that she was looked upon as "upper class," according to her black contemporaries. Several said they didn't warm to her "because she could be snooty. And she loved to have her picture in the paper." Newspaper photographs—boarding a plane with the Nine or sitting with New York Governor Averell Harriman and his wife in New York City—record her wearing a handsome fur coat and elegantly designed dresses and jewelry. I only remembered vaguely the woman I had met at my parents' home. And I remembered my deaf brother Jonathan's amazement as he told me about his introduction to her. He had brought home his deaf fiancée, Dorothy. My father had driven Daisy Bates over to the house for a meeting. My father quickly introduced Jonathan to her and without any ado, instead of shaking Jonathan's hand, she gave him a big hug. My father left them in order to answer the telephone. In walked the young, shy fiancée. According to Jonathan, Daisy Bates just went over and broke through the walls of shyness and deafness by throwing her arms around Dorothy. No gesture could have opened the gates of warmth and affection more appropriately. Jonathan said, "You do not do that with hearing people, but with deaf people she expressed herself perfectly. Very few people would have done that. It was perfect." I also remembered quite an opposite reaction to her, in a legal situation not a family situation, to be sure. A white lawyer who worked with her said to me: "Daisy Bates was steely-eyed. You didn't cross her." Yes, my father had said something like that, too.

I walked on into the museum, turned a corner, and suddenly I was startled to face a huge blow-up of a long-familiar newspaper photo. The front-page headline of the *Arkansas Democrat* evening edition of September 4, 1957, read: "Negro Students, Blocked by Guard, May Try Again." The story reported "the group of seven Negroes, assembled at 13th and Park, marched in a group to the school corner of 14th and Park. They were led by a well-dressed white man in a light suit." It was the newspaper photo my father had sent to me in Munich, marked, "THIS IS D.H.O. JR. YOUR DAD!" Never would it have occurred to the newspaper writer that for later generations sensitized to racial stereotypes his description of my father leading the black students might hint at condescension on my father's part. My father abhorred condescending attitudes, and anyone seeming to him to be acting in that way would make him tighten up. Face to face with such a person, I could always feel the edge of anger enter his voice.

In 1962 a newspaper reporter from the Charleston, West Virginia, *Gazette-Mail* sketched the only full personal impression of him I have ever found.[1]

> He is not an imposing man physically. He is neither tall nor short, fat nor thin. Ordinarily, he speaks softly; always in a Southern drawl. He uses the phrase "just a little Presbyterian minister" to describe himself and, indeed, it must have seemed to him that he was an ordinary man caught in an extraordinary situation.

I walked over to Central High. A mass of humanity in shirt sleeves and floppy sun hats spread across the lawns, from Park Street

President Bill Clinton addresses crowd, Central High integration celebration, fortieth anniversary, 1997. (Photograph by Will Counts.)

a hundred yards all the way to the school. I sat on an embankment in my assigned chair, next to the wife of the principal and her family. Stone steps led to the raised porch of what people in 1927, when it was built, described as the most beautiful high school in America. The president declared, "What happened here changed the course of our country forever."[2]

It had changed Bill Clinton's own life. He grew up just down the road in Hot Springs, Arkansas, eleven years old when the crisis erupted. "It was the single most formative experience of my childhood," he had told a pair of local reporters.[3]

Then up on that porch President Clinton, the governor, and the mayor turned to hold open the great doors as the Nine filed into the building from which they had been turned away forty years ago.

The Little Rock Nine at Central High, fortieth anniversary, 1997. Left to right: Melba Pattillo Beals, Elizabeth Eckford, Ernest Green, Gloria Ray Karlmark, Carlotta Walls LaNier, Terrence Roberts, Jefferson A. Thomas, Minnijean Brown Trickey, Thelma Jean Mothershed Wair. (Photograph by Will Counts.)

The festivities ended. I decided to stay on in Little Rock for a few more days to revisit my father's church and our home—perhaps to turn up more people who knew him back then—and, above all else, in order to find out more about that "strange duck" relationship between Daisy Bates and my father.

Central Presbyterian Church

Next morning I drove over to my father's former church on Arch Street.

Scruffy grass, dry in the September heat, tufted on the lot where I remembered a smooth green lawn bordering Central Presbyterian Church. On the black-and-white marquee sign in front a letter drooped here and there. The sign announced the brick building as a

Holiness church, African American, with Bishop Vernon Kennebrew its pastor. The front doors were unlocked.

I went in. Standing in the vestibule, I pushed ajar one of the double doors into the sanctuary. Wood pews sloped down to a low platform and curved slightly around it. Light filtered in through a handful of milky stained glass windows. It smelled of wooden desk and old rubber hall mat, familiar in long-used schools and rural churches. I remembered the three heavy, ornate carved wood-and-plush pulpit chairs still in place on the platform, now as then out of keeping with the simplicity of their surroundings.

Bishop Vernon Kennebrew stood down front, on floor level, speaking from a lectern about "give us this day our daily bread," about gratitude, talking freely without notes. He stood tall, trim, a middle-aged African American with hair going to white, in shirtsleeves. One person, a middle-aged black woman, sat in a front pew. Two boys, one a teenager, joined me in the vestibule. I nodded. They nodded back, then peered through the other set of double doors. Their interest lay in the man at the lectern. A printed sheet on a vestibule table noted a service each weekday at noon. Bishop Kennebrew finished his talk and, having spotted the boys, took an intermission from the service to stride up the aisle and into the vestibule. A hushed conversation with the two boys resulted in an exasperated upward roll of his eyes and a handful of change dug out of his pocket and laid in their open hands. They scooted.

Bishop Kennebrew turned to me with a smile and a handshake. I said, "I have children. I'm totally sympathetic."

He whispered, "School holiday."

I told him my name and said, "My father was pastor here once, and I have just come to see the church again."

He ushered me down front. I sat. Meanwhile a young black man had entered, twenty something, cap on backward, shiny leather pants, bright white tennis shoes—leaned his purple-glow bike against the pulpit platform and sprawled on a front pew. Bishop Kennebrew knelt at another of the pews. So did the woman. So did the newcomer. And so then did I, as Bishop Kennebrew asked God's healing blessing on a dozen members of the congregation, each by name with the specific malady, and called on God to hold His hand of justice over various state and national affairs, a list of which he enumerated with great specificity. To hold His hand over Archbishop Tutu in South Africa, and Nelson Mandela in now naming his former prison a national monument. Over both Anita Hill and Clarence Thomas. And over the three hundred workers and their families left jobless by last week's closing of the shoe plants up in Walnut Ridge and Jonesboro.

Bishop Kennebrew came to an end and to my surprise demanded, friendly and firm, that I stand at the lectern and talk about my father and Central High and the Little Rock Nine.

I did not know what to say. "My father used to be pastor of this church." The words spilled out automatically. I looked at the black audience and thought how my father would have felt standing at his old place today. I held the lectern. I listened to myself talk. I was speaking under the spell of the wood and the stained glass, containers of memories and my father's voice. It was as if I were watching myself. At the same time, it was as if I were watching my father give what he always called "a message." I looked across the pews as my father must have surveyed their rows, a sort of endgame where the emptiness grew and fewer figures remained. The young man, the woman, the bishop—people of goodwill—they did not know. Did it matter to them what I said, what had happened? I pointed up the aisle to the doors: "He went over there to Central High—." A terrible sinking filled me, a sense of futility, something on the inside disheartened. The way he must have felt when he entered his pulpit on a spring Sunday and looked out and his people had disappeared. He always called them "my people." Each Sunday on his copy of the church bulletin he recorded the exact number of people in attendance. I have all of his bulletins, with his penciled numbers. He must have determined to keep up a good face and to speak to the few who remained.

Standing there in the near-vacant church I looked down at the tilted board of the wooden lectern, where he must have run his fingers over the wood grain's every swelled line and whorl. I brushed the tiny undulations of the grain with my fingers. I had gazed at my father doing that many times. The surface invited the speaker to spread his notes there. I could see my father's hands laying out his half-sheets of white paper with his meticulously prepared notes—getting ready to speak.

When I was a boy I had watched him and listened to him preach this way for hundreds of hours. In these recent years I myself had been standing at a wooden lectern long familiar to me and spreading out my own half-sheets of white paper with my own meticulously prepared notes in order to talk to university classes. It struck me in that moment just how exactly I had been imitating him.

I told the audience what he had done at Central High. But, I said, people in his congregation did not agree with him, and they forced him to resign. I left it at that. Something inside me said, "Do not stir up old hostilities." More than that, why make out a white man to be a martyr when so many in the black community had suffered? And most importantly, the thought went through my head that here was a fine man, this Bishop Kennebrew, trying to keep a small congregation together and what could I do in this moment to help him? So I told the folks there what a victory the graduation of Ernest Green was both for the church and for the school. And I said that school and church working together can make a difference. And that black groups and white groups working together can make a difference.

I thought about how surprised I had been when I returned from Germany and went to hear my father preach. Of course he had grown older, but what startled me was a radical change in his presence from my boyhood days. During 1957–1958, when I had been away and the Little Rock crisis had occurred, my father the preacher had come into a new, personal age. The striking juxtapositions between his pulpit messages and his acts of courage had brought about a development in him. But it took another seven years after Little Rock before he arrived at a distillation of Jesus's life that would enable him to deliver his core message. He called it "Following in Divine Footsteps."

His notes for the sermon do not appear as usual on eight or a dozen half-sheets handwritten, front and back, but all on the front of a single eight-and-a-half-by-eleven-inch sheet of paper. He hand-prints phrases, arranging them roughly in each of nine boxes drawn on the page. The phrases are for jogging the memory, not for precise statement. Nowhere does he write, as he had in earlier days, "I read this word for word lest I be misquoted." No scholar's exegesis appears. No alternate texts or full lectionary readings occur. The single sentence of his biblical text is divided into four lines like a poem, with about two inches on the page between each of the lines.

For that climactic sermon, he selected his text from Luke 9:23:

If any man would come after me,
Let him deny himself
And take up his cross daily
And follow me.

He had an urgent, immediate message to deliver. He rarely glanced down at his notes. He talked directly about names, dates, and places of racial crisis. He went beyond Jesus's teachings. When Jesus said, "Follow me," my father asked not, "What was he saying?" but, "Where was he *going*?" It was the mandate of Jesus's actions that he linked to the necessity for actions by Christians. And he spoke with a new sound.

But there at Central Presbyterian in Little Rock, his dwindling congregation never heard that sound.

I thanked my hearers "for recalling with me a former pastor," and I stepped away from the lectern. Bishop Kennebrew said the benediction that binds us all: "May the Lord bless thee and keep thee, the Lord make his face to shine upon thee, and be gracious unto thee, the Lord lift up his countenance upon thee, and give thee peace." I heard my father's voice intoning the very same words at the end of every service, a vocal palimpsest, one Southern voice in the present laid over a Southern voice from the past. I also heard something inside me saying the words along with Bishop Kennebrew, whispering them to my father's spirit now present in this noon-lit place.

Yes. I do recall hearing your father's name," said Bishop Kennebrew after the service. "I seem to remember we had some books of his." We climbed into an attic, bumped our way through piles of dust and a couple of ancient photocopy machines. Back up under the eaves, he stepped through a door and rummaged in the dark and brought out a dusty old Presbyterian hymnal. My father's name was on the title page.

"Want it?" he asked. I didn't.

Outside, saying our farewells, he asked, "Was your father from the South?"

"He was born in Columbus, Mississippi."

Bishop Kennebrew said, "That's right near where I went to school, at Mississippi State University, in Starkville, about twenty miles west of Columbus."

Something popped into my head about my Grandmother Ogden. I said, "That a fact? My grandmother went to—it's called now Mississippi University for Women—in Columbus. She was born there."

He replied, "Back then in your grandmother's day, her college in Columbus was called the Industrial Institute and College. Funded by the state of Mississippi. It was originally founded for women, would you believe? Still is. And it's integrated. You know, at my Mississippi State University I was in the second integrated graduating class."

"So you knew all about the harassment that the Little Rock Nine talk about."

"Oh, yes. Sure enough. I have my scars," he said good-naturedly.

"Ever go back?"

"Sometimes. We stay with relatives or friends." The thought ran through my mind that black people would not have been served in restaurants or allowed to overnight in motels and hotels. Black travelers always stayed with relatives or friends.

Then we walked across the street and looked over at the church. After half a century, a black pastor schooled near the town of Columbus, Mississippi, had replaced a white pastor born in that town. We shook hands, the bishop and I, the inheritors, on a corner in a now 85 percent black neighborhood. Half a century ago, Central Presbyterian there on Arch Street had stood in the center of an all-white neighborhood: an all-white church. Calling itself "the friendly neighborhood church," it still was. My father had fought for integration. His church members had fired him because they were afraid that blacks would move into their neighborhood. Now a black Holiness congregation owned his very church. The Presbyterians had sold it in 1971. Black families now dominated his very neighborhood.

Just down the street from this Holiness church stands the black Presbyterian church of Little Rock. It was once a struggling so-called "mission church" that my father had taken under his wing. Today that black Presbyterian congregation thrives in a handsome new wood-and-glass sanctuary, its black pastor, Marion A. Humphrey, a Princeton graduate and an elected circuit court judge.

In 1956 the Christian Ministerial Alliance of black clergymen had melded with the city's organization of white clergy, the Ministerial

Central High cheerleaders, 1999. (Photograph by Will Counts.)

Association. "That in itself was a sort of a miracle," said my father. Thereafter it was the tension of the early integration days that held the interracial Ministerial Association together. Within this biracial association a group of white ministers and a group of black ministers exchanged ideas, and from it they issued statements and exerted pro-integration pressure. When the crisis passed, in the 1960s, black and white association members segregated themselves more and more, tending to join in distinct groups during their meetings and eventually sitting in clusters separated from each other during lunch. The organization became impotent and eventually died; and in its place, in 1982, the Interfaith Conference was founded by the Arkansas Council of Churches in order to accommodate Muslims and Jews. Back in 1956, as a condition of their joining in the association, the black clergy had demanded that the two rabbi members withdraw because the black clergy called themselves the "Christian Ministerial Alliance," and the two rabbis quietly did so.

A few blocks farther along from the new black Presbyterian church, one could walk through the Central High doors into the shout and push of black and white students, now as then numbering some two thousand. Basketball and football teams, the cheerleading squad, the senior prom—all appear in black and white. Black students make up 60 percent of the student body.

1863 Chester Street

We had lived several blocks away from my father's Central Presbyterian Church, at 1863 Chester Street. Forty years later the house looked so small. Next door, where a garage had been, a dozen or so derelict hulks of cars and pickups lay around. Peeling white stucco walls of the filling station were collapsing in on each other. Dust blanketed a gray fuzz over the automotive ruin. I pulled into the driveway beside the remains of a board fence that had once separated our yard from the cars. Years ago someone had painted a brick-red glaze over the housefront bricks and laid down a now moldy indoor-outdoor green carpet on the cement porch. A heavy black-iron-grille door now protected the front door.

I rang. Silence. I looked at my watch. 2:00 p.m. As I turned to walk away, the door cracked, then opened. A black man in white tank top looked at me, not unfriendly. "I'm really sorry to bother you, but I've come all the way from California. A long time ago we lived in this house. I just couldn't help wanting to see it. Could I look inside? For just a minute?" He nodded, shifted his beer to the other hand, and pulled the door open a little wider. I stepped into the gloom. He could slam the door, tie me up, take my wallet, no one would hear a sound. Would he? They? Was someone else in the house? My racist fears lingered. His sheeted couch-bed stood on one side of the room, the television on, on the other. A dim light in the dining room.

All at once I could see our chairs all around the walls. And I could hear ten, twenty reporters talking, some of them dark skinned. My father at one side, explaining, delivering information, naming names, giving views. "There are wrong attitudes between these two groups of people in the South," he was saying. "It is as if these attitudes were moisture in suspension in the air. The climate has changed in Little Rock, precipitation has followed, and the chill rain falls." The reporters were writing on their pads, coffee cups on the floor and tables. My mother serving coffee. The clock reading midnight. The only places in town the out-of-town reporters could gather, black and white together, were our home and the Bateses' house. That's why *Time* and the *New York Times* quoted my father. "The black race and the white race . . . separated by a glass wall. . . . ," he once told them. He made good copy. He was a man of vivid images and scrupulous accuracy, with a formidable memory, and he was in black homes as much as in white, so he knew what was going on at the grassroots level.

The former pastor of Second Presbyterian had said to me, "We ministers used to have a joke about your father. Whenever a displaced person would come to town—a Japanese, someone like that—the first question he would ask was, 'Where is Dunbar Ogden? Do you know Dunbar Ogden?' Of course we told that joke in love, but you know, he even went and visited people in the YMCA!" During World War II, a Japanese internment camp had been set up near Little Rock. Sometimes people went from there to the YMCA, and my father would try to help get them jobs and a more permanent place to stay.

Standing there in that television half-light I saw our couch over by the window. The living room was much smaller than I had remembered it. I could hear crying. Suddenly my younger brother David was sitting there on the couch—he was bigger than the rest of us at six foot one—with his hands sort of hanging down by his sides, his head bent forward, tears running down his cheeks. The stresses of that integration year had gotten to him. The tears wouldn't stop. It was midnight. He just kept sitting there and crying, not moving or anything. He was twenty-one or twenty-two.

I saw through to the dining room, my father seated on a chair at one end of the table in his pajamas and bathrobe, old slippers, reading the Bible out loud, now and then raising his head to explain a passage to us.

David and I sat at the table pouring cornflakes onto our hot oatmeal and wolfing down breakfast, our attention on getting out the door, while he took his ritual ten minutes to let us hear the King James.

"Mama," the young black man called. Around the corner from what I knew to be the hall into the front bedroom came a black woman, probably in her seventies, supporting her bloated body on a walker and clumping into the dining room to collapse on a chair. Perspiration beginning to drip from her temples. Panting and aching. Not unfriendly. I dared turn sideways, half away from the young black man in order to hear her.

"Ye-ah. Some people say white folks did use to live here. Long time ago. I don't know."

"I used to sleep right there in that front bedroom. I'm sorry for coming in here all of a sudden on you like this, I don't want to be a bother to you, but I was wondering if I could just look at the room where I slept, just to remember?" That was the bedroom the Reverend Charles C. Walker from the black Congregational Church had warned my mother to get everybody out of. He had lived down the street.

"Mama" looked over her shoulder toward the bedroom. "I can't let you go in there. It ain't made up. It's all mess up and ever'thing." She was embarrassed. So was I. The telephone was ringing. I thanked them and closed the front door behind me.

Why had I conjured up my brother David sitting on the Chester Street living-room couch, arms hanging by his side, crying? As I stood there on the porch, the telephone inside the house was still ringing. Sometimes when I am outside our house and I hear a phone ringing inside, and I jam and twist the key in the door lock to rush in and answer it, I remember being at Yale and coming home to our New Haven apartment and jamming my key in the door lock and opening the door to pick up the ringing phone—to hear something in my father's voice I had never heard before.

It was about David.

David

On June 23, 1960, my father was calling me in New Haven from my parents' home in Huntington, West Virginia, to tell me what had happened. My brother David had driven to Rogersville, Tennessee, where he had taken a motel room. There he wrote a letter to my father and mother and a letter to each of us three brothers. He smoked a pack of cigarettes through the night, pounded a nail into the top of a wooden footstool, sat on the floor with his back to the bed, loaded a shotgun, drew his knees up to his chest, put his feet against the stool, laid the butt of the gun on the stool, put the trigger against the upright nail, placed the muzzle against his chest, and with his feet pushed the stool away from him, jamming the nail against the trigger and firing a hole about the size of a silver dollar into his chest. "The police said he died instantly," said my father.

My brother David had been a year younger than I. We had grown up always a pair in the family, the two of us lying awake at night in our separate beds deciding which baseball gloves we'd buy from Sears, or pushing our bikes out of the garage in the dark at 5:00 a.m. to pick up our newspapers for our paper routes, or throwing walnuts at each other, or punching each other in the backseat of the family car on every trip.

Under circumstances of great emotional stress it was always my father's way to explain with all details. On the phone my father tried to keep his voice level. He had to stop sometimes. "No, your mother can't talk on the telephone now. She's upstairs." I knew she would cry if she got on the phone. She did not want me to hear her crying.

Before the service at the funeral home, in Springfield, Ohio (my mother's family home), I found my father standing by himself at the open casket looking into David's face and reaching in with both hands to hold David's folded hands. He was saying, out loud, "Why did you do it, my son? Why did you do it?" I went over and put my hand on his shoulder. All I could think to say was, "Don't torture yourself, Dad, don't torture yourself." Comforting him wrenched me. And suddenly I saw an awful kind of shape to these events.

My father deeply felt the vulnerability of his deaf sons, Jonathan and Paul. I looked over at them, now sitting on metal chairs waiting for the service to start, eleven-year-old Paul patting different people on the shoulder. I had just come from distracting Paul by letting him steer my Volkswagen up and down some back roads. Earlier I had gotten in a heated argument with the tombstone maker about the punctuation he was proposing to chisel in the inscription. A residue of the anger still stuck in my throat. That was my way under extreme emotional strain. It still is: to fasten on a petty detail, something that I think is an error, and to pick a quarrel about it. My mother had laid her hand on my arm and said softly, "It's all right. Let it go." And I did.

My father, I thought, expected me as the oldest to be strong, just as his parents had expected him as the oldest to be strong. From David, too, he had expected an inner toughness—from both of us, a kind of elasticity and resistance. In a strange way my father climbed out of depression with Little Rock, while Little Rock plunged David into it. My father felt great ambivalence toward other people who were suffering from depression, just as he felt great ambivalence about himself. Perhaps this is why David as a depressed person turned out to be the last person my father was capable of helping—and the one, above all, whom he most wanted to save.

After the funeral I drove my father to Rogersville to pick up David's car. On the way, my father said, "I have the receipt from the pawn shop where he bought the shotgun. I found it in his car. I never want to see that gun again. I threw it away." A church member had driven my father to identify the body and inspect the motel room. "The cigarette butts," my father told me. "There were exactly nineteen cigarette butts in the toilet. I counted them. He smoked each cigarette in the pack and when the last one was finished in the early morning, he did it." A pack had twenty cigarettes. I held the wheel and stared at the road. Numb. My father sitting beside me. The two of us. If ever I have breathed the short-breath air at the breaking of a heart, that was it.

As with my father, depression had struck David suddenly and hard, at age twenty—approximately the same age as it had first hit my father. At twenty David graduated from Southwestern College in Memphis, Tennessee. When my parents left Little Rock, he stayed behind. He had a job with an auto parts company. Fellow workers discovered what his father had done and besieged him—first with taunts of "you nigger lover" and "If you love Daisy Bates so much, why don't you wear a daisy?" Eventually came physical attacks. At home a black cleaning woman would not come in and clean his apartment for fear of retaliation. He quit, took another job, was soon found out, and the pattern repeated itself. David drove to West Virginia and joined my parents. He was despondent. On June 22, 1960, he drove to the Tennessee motel—on his way to see friends, he had said—and early the next morning took his own life. He was twenty-four.

David's story is the only part of the Little Rock experience that my father and my mother could never be reconciled with. In certain moods my father would repeat to me, "I killed my own son. Sometimes I feel guilty as hell," he would say.

In his last years, every now and then when the two of us would be walking along or driving somewhere, he would pause and lay out his convictions for me—simple, brief, straightforward, wanting no answer—as if fixing them in himself. But never once, after I left home for college, did my father ever ask me about my religious beliefs, and, as I drifted away from organized religion, never once did he make the slightest attempt to persuade me to any of his views. In those moments, almost talking to himself, he would say yes, he did believe in a personal God. Yes, he did believe in "our Lord Jesus Christ." Yes, he did believe in some kind of life after death. Through a lifetime of doubts more faith-shaking than any of his parishioners could have imagined, he had come to a few solid convictions. He knew his end was near, and he wanted to impress them on me, privately and unalterably. These moments were always spontaneous. We would just happen to be alone, and I could tell that something was on his mind. A few months before he died, he did it once again. He was often talking about Little Rock then. He said, "When I look back at my life, I regret nothing. Nothing. I have no regrets." His voice was strong, emphatic, militant. Then he would pause. His voice would soften and crack: "Except the death of David. Except the death of David."

My mother believed that at her death, David and my father would be standing in heaven, whatever that was, welcoming her with open arms.

Daisy Bates

Now walking down the cement walk away from my 1997 anniversary visit to our old home on Chester Street, I remembered that the last person I knew who had seen David alive in Little Rock was Daisy Bates. More than anyone else, I wanted to talk with her, who, according to my father, was once "the most hated woman in town." I had met her long ago, once or twice. I had written ahead. Then as soon as I had arrived in Little Rock for the celebration, I had telephoned and spoken first with Gene Gentry, her caregiver and driver. "I cannot tell you how important you are to her," he said. "Without Dunbar Ogden she would not have had the strength, the moral support. Through his sacrifices. He was the most instrumental person to her. When he left that was truly a loss for her. There was a resource of strength that she was able to pull from him. Her white motivation [motivating force from the white community] was very important for her. It was a great loss when your family left town. A third leg had been knocked out from under the milking stool. She never got over it. She brings him up all the time."

Where my father had lost his church, she—together with her husband—had lost her newspaper. An economic backlash had hit Little Rock as a direct result of the civil rights upheaval. Nat Griswold, head of the Arkansas Council on Human Relations, reported that "as an aftermath of the crisis at Central High School . . . from 1958 to 1961 the city added not a single new industry."[4]

Meanwhile the Bateses reported that advertisements in the *State Press* had fallen off by 75 percent during the first year of the integration crisis. They launched a campaign for support from local black clergy but garnered only a handful of new subscriptions. They had to raise the price from ten to fifteen cents.

From their beginning, May 9, 1941, they continued to feature on the masthead their original mission: "to integrate the Negro in all phases of community activities as American citizens." But in the spring of 1958 they announced, "We don't have a record of any religious, fraternal or civic leader in Little Rock asking his followers to support the *State Press*." In their view the black community did not rally behind them.

During 1958–1959 they hung on, managed to support the new Women's Emergency Committee and the seven remaining members of the Nine, who, like all other high school students in Little Rock, scrambled to find a high school somewhere. The Bateses fought in the vanguard to get the schools reopened. In the fall of 1959, Little Rock's high schools were functioning again. Carlotta Walls and Jefferson Thomas re-entered Central High, where they would graduate in May 1960. Three new black students entered Hall High School. In addition, three new black students were admitted to Central High (including the son of the Rev. Franklin Henderson, my father's black associate). On opening day Police Chief Gene Smith with "a hundred of my best men" armed with nightsticks fought off a rioting mob of an estimated one thousand at the grounds of Central High. There had already been drive-by shootings. Eventually the city police had to use fire hoses to get control. They arrested nineteen.

The debate and the reactions that should have occurred two years earlier did occur in the fall of 1959. In the fall of 1957, the reality of school integration sprang in the faces of Little Rock's citizenry. Its yes-or-no immediacy—yes, these nine enter Central High today, or no, they don't—took them by surprise. If asked what they thought, most readers of the *State Press*, the *Gazette*, and the *Democrat* and most

School integration protesters march at Arkansas State
Capitol, Little Rock. (Photograph by Will Counts.)

members of my father's congregation simply had not had time to consider. Would it mean a huge alteration in their status quo? They were totally unprepared to answer the question.

Two years later, at the beginning of the 1959 school year, the bravery of black students finally became part of the discussion. The role of the black press grew strong as a locus for information and debate. School board members in Little Rock could take solid positions because they knew what they stood for. The job of the police to protect became abundantly clear. Clergy, white and black, chose deliberately what they would and would not do. They knew specifically what confronted members of their congregations. For example, Rufus King Young, the pastor of Bethel AME, could make up his mind to take a vigorous, out-in-the-open pro-school-integration stance, whereas the white head of the Southern Baptist Church with his "go-slow" insistence faced off directly against the NAACP.

In Little Rock during 1958–1959, the Women's Emergency Committee formed to clean up what they saw as the men's mess and force open the schools. The organizers included no black women. Mrs. Adolphine Terry, widow of U.S. Congressman Dave Terry, led the WEC. In February 1958, her indoctrination had begun when she became a regular in the Thursday Group. But a black-white action group for social change still remained an instrument of the future.

Now tokenism stood uncovered, no longer able to hide minimal grudging lawfulness. Downtown the Chamber of Commerce could declare publicly that Little Rock was suddenly falling into an economic backslide. No new industries wished to plant themselves on such unstable ground.

Perhaps most important, public dialogue rather than private whisper started to articulate a cleaner sense of socioeconomic class. While over at Central High, billy clubs and fire hoses had to put down integration riots because of the neighborhood, Hall High School integrated peacefully because it stood in a better part of town. The people beaten in the eruptions were black adults. Blacks were still beaten up for protesting. To blacks in Little Rock, as all over Dixie, "gradual" meant "token," "later" meant "never," and "go slow" meant "no."

In their paper the Bateses countered fiercely the written requests by sixty-three white students at Central High and five at Hall High that they not be forced to sit in the same classroom with any black students. The requests were honored by the school officials. The Bateses in their October 30, 1959, issue quoted Harry Truman saying that if he'd been president in 1957, "I'd have put Faubus and the whole gang in jail." They reported on the same page the theft of their safe, later found emptied of $90.

That was it. Without ceremony, after nineteen years of operation uninterrupted—they were proud of that—Daisy and L. C. Bates closed down their *State Press.*

The last days of Police Chief Gene Smith passed more tragically. It was he and his men who had taken control of a rioting mob at the grounds of Central High when school had opened in the fall of 1959. He had given protection to the entering black students, as he had promised Daisy Bates. But the pressures of the confrontations were finally getting to him. Then on March 18, 1960, his son was convicted of a series of thefts in Searcy, Arkansas. It pushed him over the edge. That evening he killed his wife and then himself.

Where Gene Smith's end shook Daisy Bates, my brother David's suicide in June 1960 shaped in a graphic way her view of my father and their 1957–1958 experience as she looked back on it. Her "children," as she called the Nine, had all survived. His son had not. Then, as she set about writing her book, published in 1962, her attitude toward my father changed once again. The process of writing the book jolted in her a new understanding of my father and impelled her to put it into words for herself.[5]

While driving the streets to Daisy Bates's house, it occurred to me that during my interviews with my father, I had always heard him refer to her as "Mrs. Bates," never calling her "Daisy Bates" unless he was naming her among other civil rights pioneers. White people in the South often called black adults by their first name. Not my father. That was a scrupulous point with him. Every adult he met was to him a "Mr." or "Mrs.," no matter in what social or economic position.

Perhaps in doing that he confused people. In making casual introductions on the street and at formal public occasions, it certainly set him apart from other white Southerners. Southerners regarded outsiders as suspect, and in crisis situations they tolerated no dissent and yielded to no influence if they perceived it as coming from outsiders. In that sense both my father and Daisy Bates confused people around them. Each could be called a solid insider: my father from an old, plantation-owning family, born in Columbus, Mississippi, and his father one of the most highly respected men among Southern clergy who had served distinguished churches in what sounds like a geography lesson in great old Deep South cities: Knoxville, Atlanta, Louisville, Mobile, and New Orleans.

Daisy Bates provided an exact counterpart. Born and raised in Huttig, Arkansas, she came right from native rural roots. As of 1941, the Bates newspaper sounded *the* public voice for black Little Rock. Yet both Daisy Bates and my father conducted themselves in unorthodox ways, each like an outsider. They both opposed white and black orthodoxy, and as a result raised the hackles of a lot of people in their respective communities.

I was struck by the coincidences in this Little Rock story. I saw how things had merged to bring about this integration: Daisy Bates's courage, my father's empathy, the black students' desire to go to college. Perhaps that's a major characteristic of history: ironic accident.

I had only the vaguest memory of Daisy Bates. I found the house and pulled up in the car. There stood the modest fifties-style bungalow with its carport at one end and the famous plate-glass window in the middle, hot sun glancing off its smooth surface. I sat for a moment, imagining the chicken wire and crisscrosses of duct tape that once held it together. And I thought about sinister automobiles cruising this street at night, with their lights off. About L. C. Bates clambering along the roof water-hosing out a Molotov cocktail fire. About KKK crosses burning on the now heat-dried grass in front. About Daisy Bates sitting inside the doorway with a shotgun across her lap. What did she have to tell me about my father?

Her caregiver Gene Gentry let me in and ushered me into the living room. The walls were covered with plaques honoring her, more plaques than wallpaper. And a handful of photographs of her with U.S. presidents: Eisenhower, Kennedy, Johnson, Nixon, Ford, Carter, Clinton. I glanced over at the famous picture window. There was no spiderweb of cracks. She was getting around in a wheelchair. Head still high. Elegant hair. Not an ounce of fat. Hands that had grasped big objects, had pointed with authority, and had pounded a typewriter. Large glasses rounded what her opponents used to call "those steely eyes." Several small strokes had slightly impaired her speech. I perched on the edge of a couch so I could look directly into her face. When she spoke, she spoke in paragraphs.

"He was a man among men," was about the first thing she said to me. I think she had rehearsed that often. Over time the sentence had taken on great import in her mind.

"What does that mean?" I asked her. Clearly she had used the phrase on many occasions.

She paused, turning it over in her mind, before she answered. "He was a man of his word. You could trust every word he said. I have met no one like him. He was a man of God. I have met many ministers. He was a Christian. He gave me courage."

"What brought him to do what he did?"

"He was a true man of God."

I had not anticipated that she of all people would immediately begin talking about God and about "being a Christian." During the past forty years, between the Central High integration and its anniversary, she had fought many local battles in the avant-garde of civil rights. On the national scene, she had appeared at nearly every event where the civil rights pioneers gathered—with Rosa Parks, Thurgood Marshall, and often, after King's untimely death, with the succeeding leaders Roy Wilkins and Ralph Abernathy. Her husband, thirteen years her senior, had died in 1980. Her skirmishes with black clergy continued. I now think that in those intervening years she had arrived at an awareness of the unique role my father had played in her life—and of how brief the 1957–1958 moment had been.

Sitting there in her living room with me, she began talking about her present dilemmas. Perhaps I reminded her a little of my father. "If I have friends who are not of color, why is there suspicion?" she said suddenly, looking me in the eye. "There's a feeling in the black community that if people are to work with me, they should be black." The commemoration ceremony was much on her mind. I was surprised at how she confided in me. She said, "I think I have done something I should not have done." She talked about her "signing over rights to [anniversary] T-shirts and profits from the sale of the book." *The Long Shadow* had just been reissued for the anniversary.

Perhaps, she thought, she could have directed the profits to a worthy cause under her control.

She remained still for a while, alert and upright in her wheelchair that sunny afternoon. Recalling my father again, she told me she had a deep belief in God. She said she believed she was here on earth for a purpose. As to organized religion, she was not comfortable and never had been, but, she went on, "Now, I need to get back into church."

"Why did you call my father that night?" I asked her.

"The children needed someone to believe in."

"But he was white."

"We knew that. We had called all over. We had called ten black ministers and they had turned us down. Your father generated a kind of different feeling and relief that they needed." For the first time she turned her head away from me—I had been sitting looking directly into her face—and she stared up where a man might stand beside her. "I can see him now, your father. My husband was not much of a religious man, but your father, you could talk to him. Now, whenever I think of him, I get a warm feeling." She was smiling to herself, hugging herself a little, pulling her shoulders together in a cozy-by-the-fire gesture.

I said, "Martin Luther King and Gandhi, they did not do things for *other* people. They led struggles for their *own* people. What my father did was different. It was for *others*, not for his own family or race or group."

"I don't think Dunbar Ogden looked at the children as belonging to a race. He looked at people in need. He didn't see people in black and white."

"What about Governor Faubus? You met him."

"A lot of people have asked me, 'How could you forgive Faubus? How could you look him in the eye?' 'Faubus,' I said, 'was reared with segregation. He had this steeped in him. We need to educate the parents. They were only doing what they were taught. Before that Faubus didn't even recognize blacks. Those people were slaves, and the whites didn't think anything about it.' "

I asked her, "Did my father teach you anything?"

"Your father, the *way* he taught. Your father, I felt he was all right. He taught by his actions. He'd never say, 'Here comes a nigger.' That just wasn't in him."

"Did you teach my father anything?"

"No. He taught me."

"When black and white ministers took no action, how did they justify their inaction?"

"It was *fear*. A white church lady was complaining to me one day about segregation and racism, and I said, 'Why don't you *do* something?' And she said to me, 'Mrs. Bates, you're asking too much.' "

"Was there any other person who was a comrade to you, besides your husband, L. C. Bates, and Dunbar Ogden, not just a friend or even a close friend, but a comrade in the crisis?"

"No."[6]

Back in my Little Rock hotel room I thought over my afternoon with "Mrs. Bates." In my mind's ear I could hear my father talking about her as "Mrs. Bates." I asked myself: As the crisis developed, had my father in some strange way fit a profile of a fellow worker Daisy Bates had wished for, perhaps more unconsciously than consciously? I knew she had written in her book that when she was four years old, three white men had raped and murdered her mother in Huttig, Arkansas. And I knew from her newspaper that she had little truck with organized religion, and in her eyes local black pastors always let her down or directly opposed her. Could she in truth ever have conceived of a white man as her collaborator, not only that but a white clergyman?

When the Little Rock crisis broke, Daisy Bates was almost forty-three or forty-four, and my father was fifty-five. Bates was at the height of her physical and mental powers; my father in top form, vigorous again after the nervous breakdown in 1951. They had in common a deep Christian faith and a healthy skepticism toward whites and blacks as do-gooders—and toward organized religion.

Was she aware in those months of the uniqueness of my father's role for her? She began to express an awareness publicly in 1962 with the appearance of *The Long Shadow of Little Rock*. "At the height of the Little Rock crisis," she wrote, "few white citizens came forward in support of law and order."

Through the operation of the *State Press*, she and L. C. Bates knew a great deal about labor and labor unions. "Not one labor leader, for example, spoke out." As to churches, "Initially, several ministers voiced their approval of a peaceful fulfillment of the school board's integration plan. But, as the battle lines were gathered, they became silent. A single exception was the Reverend Dunbar Ogden, who continued to address himself to the conscience of Little Rock."[7]

I came to the conclusion that it was after my father left Little Rock that Daisy Bates began to take full cognizance of what he had done and its consequences. No other minister, black or white, had lost his church because of the upheaval. And then the suicide of my brother David in 1960, I think, shocked Daisy Bates into full recognition of who my father was—who his family was—and what they had gone through. No other parents, black or white, had lost a child in the crisis.

Musing over my visit with Daisy Bates, I found myself making a mental ledger, comparing her with my father, thinking about how different they were and how they must have regarded each other. On my father's side of this mental ledger, as the 1957–1958 crisis developed, it seemed to me that Daisy Bates represented someone my father had long wished for, though he never clearly defined for himself such a person—some kindred spirit in one of his congregations or some like-minded colleague in one of his controversial church or civic projects. In a sense he had always been a loner. Furthermore, Daisy Bates seemed an unlikely partner in battle for my father: for him her characteristics ranged from problematic to off-putting. She was a woman; she was black; she was egocentric; and she was pushy, aggressive, and outspoken. Yes, in the context of his traditional Southern upbringing she did not "know her place." Yet, as he often said to me with deep admiration in his voice and with the use of an expression he reserved only for her: "She had guts."

During my 1977 interviews with my father, he told me about the time he was passing through Little Rock after the 1957–1958 crisis was over, when he realized it was a Thursday, and on a whim, unannounced, he dropped by a meeting of the interracial Thursday Group that he and Daisy Bates had founded in support of the parents of the Nine. It was still going. He said he didn't call ahead. He just walked in. Daisy Bates ran over and threw her arms around him. "Never," my father said to me, "did I ever think that Dunbar Ogden would be kissed by Daisy Bates."

Notes

2
"Blood will run in the streets."

1. Later Colbert Cartwright made a point that he did not walk with the black students but stood at the edge of the group and then the crowd in order to see what was going on.

2. In the photograph at the rear of the group of black students stands a tall black girl named Jane Lee Hill. On September 4, 1957, she walked with the group of black students led by my father. From the 215 students at the black Horace Mann High School who signed up to transfer to Central High during 1957–1958, Superintendent Blossom selected 17. Then on the Labor Day weekend 1957, just preceding school opening, Blossom persuaded 8 of the 17 to back out, leaving the Nine. He promised them they could transfer later. He did not keep the promise. Jane Lee Hill had not been one of the 17 selected, but she still decided to try to enter Central High. After the events of September 4, 1957, she returned to Horace Mann. Roy Reed, *Faubus* (Fayetteville: University of Arkansas Press, 1997), 209. *State Press,* August 22, 1958.

3. The preceding narrative is based on my interviews with my father, and on interviews by Don Marsh with my father, published in the Charleston, West Virginia, *Gazette-Mail*, "Rev. Ogden's Cruel Dilemma at Little Rock," December 16, 1962, together with my father's penciled notes (December 3, 1962) on a transcript of the Marsh interviews.

4. Unpublished book-length autobiography by Colbert S. Cartwright, "Walking My Lonesome Valley," Fort Worth, Texas, 1993, 112.

5. Cartwright, "Walking," 127.

6. Elizabeth Huckaby, *Crisis at Central High* (Baton Rouge: University of Louisiana Press, 1980), 72, 85, 95.

7. I have followed the practice of almost all contemporary sources in writing "Mothers League" without an apostrophe (i.e., Mothers' League).

8. Staff correspondent [Anne Braden], "Little Rock Climaxes Spiritual Journey," *Southern Patriot*, 17, no. 7 (September 1959).

9. Eleanor Roosevelt, "Courage in Little Rock," *Boston Daily Globe*, 1958, quoted in the *State Press*, 19, no. 15 (August 28, 1959), 5.

10. Nat R. Griswold, "The Second Reconstruction in Little Rock," unpublished book-length manuscript, Sparkman, Arkansas, ca. 1969–1970, book 2, chapter 6, 23. Griswold attended many Thursday Group gatherings.

11. Daisy Bates, *The Long Shadow of Little Rock* (New York: David McKay, 1962), 86, 182. Did they drive first to the home of Daisy and L. C. Bates? After the arrival of the 101st Airborne, the Nine would meet before and after school at the Bateses' home. Usually the military escort picked them up and dropped them off there each day, sometimes varying the routine with pick-up at a parents' home in order to avoid attack.

12. Ernest Q. Campbell and Thomas F. Pettigrew wrote that my father "praised the move" and that he was "the only one." ("A Study in Courage," *Christianity and Crisis*, 18, no. 16 [September 29, 1958], 134, 136).

13. It was from her bodyguard, Danny, that Melba Pattillo Beals got the title of her book, *Warriors Don't Cry* (New York: Simon and Schuster, 1994), 161. At the end of September 30, a day filled with little cruelties, Danny had told her, "In order to get through this year you will have to become a soldier. Never let your enemy know what you are feeling."

14. Anne Braden, *The Wall Between* (New York: Monthly Review Press, 1958), recounts the fury unleashed against the Bradens, and against a black family, when in the spring of 1954 the Bradens sold their house in a white suburb of Louisville, Kentucky, to a black family. Anne and Karl Braden visited my parents on several occasions. Anne inscribed a copy of her book to them: "You are proving under fire the power of Christianity at its best."

    Meanwhile Lorraine Hansberry was writing *A Raisin in the Sun*, where at the end of the play, the black family moves into a white neighborhood. The drama, the *State Press* would report to its readers, opened on Broadway in the fall of 1959. Daisy Bates and Lorraine Hansberry would become friends.

15. Campbell and Pettigrew, "A Study in Courage." See also Ernest Q. Campbell and Thomas F. Pettigrew, *Christians in Racial Crisis, a Study of Little Rock's Ministry* (Washington, DC: Public Affairs Press, 1959). See also Griswold, "Second Reconstruction," book 2, chapter 2, 19.

16. Campbell and Pettigrew, "A Study in Courage."

17. Campbell and Pettigrew, "A Study in Courage."

18. Reed, *Faubus*, 1997, 275–85.

19. Reed, *Faubus*, 245.

3

"I didn't know it could cut so deep."

1. Charleston, West Virginia, *Gazette-Mail*, December 16, 1962.
2. Elizabeth Huckaby, *Crisis at Central High* (Baton Rouge: Louisiana State University Press, 1980), 152.
3. Campbell and Pettigrew, "A Study in Courage."
4. *Arkansas Gazette*, October 6, 1957, 5F.
5. Will D. Campbell, *Race and the Renewal of the Church* (Philadelphia: Westminster Press, 1962). Author's interview with Will D. Campbell, Mt. Juliet, Tennessee, September 29, 1997.
   Citation from Isaiah 40:18–23.
6. See Beth Roy, *Bitters in the Honey* (Fayetteville: University of Arkansas Press, 1999). Forty years after these events, Beth Roy tape-recorded interviews with white alumni of Central High from the 1957–1958 period, investigating the reasons behind their resistance to desegregation.

4

"No preacher is going to run me off from my church."

1. Romans 8:28. Philippians 4:13. "In the Greek the passage reads 'I can all things,'" my father said to me. "The word 'do' is not there. I can all things—I can suffer all things, I can bear all things, I can share all things, I can impart all things."
2. It is the view of the Rev. Don Campbell that the disappearance of Central Presbyterian Session's minutes specifically and only for that period is no accident. In 1957–1958 Don Campbell was a young Presbyterian minister in Crossett, Arkansas. Ever since then he has continued to serve as a pastor in Arkansas. He has carried out an extensive search for the Session minutes. Interviews with author: Little Rock, September 24, 1997, and August 27, 2001. Correspondence with the author: September 17, 1997; February 15, 2002.
3. Griswold, "Second Reconstruction," book 2, chapter 4,13.
4. Author's telephone interview with the Rev. Richard Hardie, Little Rock, September 22, 1997.
5. Author's telephone interview with the Rev. William Fogleman, Wimberlye, Texas, October 7, 1997.
6. Griswold, "Second Reconstruction," book 5, chapter 2, 15.
7. *New York Times* , September 17, 1958, 1.
8. Bates, *The Long Shadow*, 193.

5

"He taught by his actions."

1. Don Marsh, in Charleston, West Virginia, *Gazette-Mail*, December 16, 1962.
2. Associated Press, *Arkansas Democrat-Gazette*, September 26, 1997.
3. Terry Lemons, Jane Fullerton, "A 'haunting but hopeful moment,'" *Arkansas Democrat-Gazette*, September 25, 1997, 12A–13A.

    Clinton told reporters, "I want to say one thing to you. I think it is fabulous what you guys did in reprinting all the old newspapers. I read it voraciously, and I gave it to all the people who were working with me on my speech." He went on: " . . . an old copy of *Time* magazine from September 23, 1957. And I read that."

    In his copy of *Time*, Clinton was reading my father's on-the-spot analysis. Also *Time*, 70, no. 15 (October 7, 1957), 17–21.
4. Griswold, "Second Reconstruction," book 2, chapter 3, 12.
5. Don Marsh, "Rev. Ogden's Cruel Dilemma at Little Rock," Charleston, West Virginia, *Gazette-Mail*, December 16, 1962.
6. Author's interview with Daisy Bates at her home in Little Rock, Arkansas, September 26, 1997.
7. Daisy Bates, *The Long Shadow of Little Rock* (New York: David McKay, 1962), 180. Campbell and Pettigrew, in "A Study in Courage," had called him "*the* voice of conscience for his colleagues no less than the city itself."

Index

Page numbers in **bold** indicate pictures.

and Pastor Young, 37
science project, 47
Thanksgiving dinner, **77**
workplace reprisals, 43
Reconciliation Service, 130–31
Reed, Roy, 61
Reinhardt, Max, 130
religious beliefs and principles, 22–23,
36–37, 51, 147, 155. *See also* sermons;
*individual Biblical passages; individual
churches*
retinitis pigmentosa, 65
Rickey, Branch, 79
Roaring River State Park, **6**
Roberts, Terrence, 33, 37, 48, **77, 135**. *See
also* Little Rock Nine
Robinson, Jackie, 79
Rogersville, Tennessee, 144
Romans 8:28, 159n1
Romans 17:1, 122
Roosevelt, Eleanor, 50, 85, 125
Rotary club, 84
Roy, Beth, 159n6

Saint Andrews Cathedral (Little Rock),
130
Sanders, Ira, 123, 125
scholarship fund, 43–44
Second Presbyterian, 143
segregation. *See also* Mothers League
of Central High School
boycott *State Press*, 76–77
financial impact on Little
Rock, 148, 150
Little Rock votes for, 121
mongrelization, 68
Ogden family history, 11–15
opposed by Presbyterian Church, 114
poetic justice, 69
Warren Ogden, 118
White Citizens Council, 47, 63
Selma-to-Montgomery march, 95
Senate Internal Security Subcommittee,
72
sermons
"Beyond the Law," 42
"Christ in Crisis," 38
"Christ Supreme," 22
on crisis, 51–52
"Following in Divine
Footsteps," 138–39

"Great Expectations," 75–76
"Great in the Sight of God," 83
"The Just Shall Live by Faith," 121–22
Matthew 3:47 (graduation day), 91–92
Ogden style, 38–41, 138–39
"Opportunities of a Life Time," 83
"Peace and Palm Branches," 38
sermon style, 84–85
"The Sword and the Star," 38
"The Teachings of Christ for
Our Times," 56–57
"The Will of God for Your Life," 74
"With Liberty and Justice for All: The
Danger of Rejecting Jesus," 41–42
Session (elected elders), 59, 108–9, 113,
159n2
Seventh Day Adventists, 37
Shelton, Bill, 102–3
shipwreck analogy, 76
slavery, 9, 30, 32
Sleigh, Victoria, 12
Smiley, Glenn, 85
Smith, Gene, 54, 96–97, 148, 150
Snowball, 11–12
Southern Baptist Church, 149
Southern Christian Leadership
Conference, 72
Southern Conference Educational Fund,
71–72
Southwestern College, 146
Southwestern University, 9
speech patterns, 17–18
Springarn Medal, 86
Starkville, Mississippi, 140
State Press
Arkansas Agricultural,
Mechanical and Normal
College graduation, 94
attack on journalist, 52, **53**
bankruptcy, 76–77, 105, 148, 150
and the Bates family, 1, 101–2
black apathy, 62–63, 105
Green graduation, 82
McCarthyism, 71–72
and Minnijean Brown, 73, 79, 81
Nine as front page news, 78
101st Airborne escort, 55
A Raisin in the Sun, 158n14
Springarn Medal dispute, 86
white students refuse to
sit with black, 150